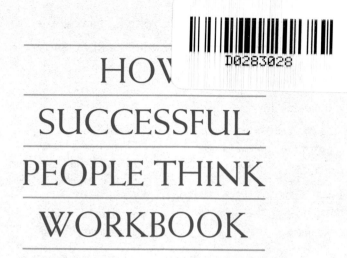

HOW SUCCESSFUL PEOPLE THINK WORKBOOK

Books by Dr. John C. Maxwell

Can Teach You How to Be a REAL Success

Relationships

25 Ways to Win with People
Becoming a Person of Influence
Encouragement Changes Everything
Ethics 101
Everyone Communicates, Few Connect
The Power of Partnership
Relationships 101
Winning with People

Attitude

Attitude 101
The Difference Maker
Failing Forward
How Successful People Think
Success 101
Thinking for a Change
The Winning Attitude

Equipping

The 17 Essential Qualities of a Team Player
The 17 Indisputable Laws of Teamwork
Developing the Leaders around You
Equipping 101
Make Today Count
Mentoring 101
My Dream Map
Partners in Prayer
Put Your Dream to the Test
Running with the Giants
Talent Is Never Enough
Today Matters
Your Road Map for Success

Leadership

The 10th Anniversary Edition of The 21 Irrefutable Laws of Leadership
The 21 Indispensable Qualities of a Leader
The 21 Most Powerful Minutes in a Leader's Day
The 360 Degree Leader
Developing the Leader within You
The Five Levels of Leadership (Fall 2011)
Go For Gold
Leadership 101
Leadership Gold
Leadership Promises for Every Day

HOW
SUCCESSFUL
PEOPLE THINK
WORKBOOK

CHANGE YOUR THINKING, CHANGE YOUR LIFE

JOHN C. MAXWELL

CENTER STREET

New York   Boston   Nashville

Copyright © 2011 by John C. Maxwell

Portions of this book were previously published in *Thinking for a Change* and *How Successful People Think* by John C. Maxwell.

The author is represented by Yates & Yates, LLP, Literary Agency, Orange, California.

Center Street
Hachette Book Group
1290 Avenue of the Americas
New York, NY 10104
www.centerstreet.com

Center Street is a division of Hachette Book Group, Inc. The Center Street name and logo are trademarks of Hachette Book Group, Inc.

The publisher is not responsible for websites (or their content) that are not owned by the publisher.

The Hachette Speakers Bureau provides a wide range of authors for speaking events. To find out more, go to www.hachettespeakersbureau.com or call (866) 376-6591.

Printed in the United States of America

First Edition: June 2011

12

Library of Congress Cataloging-in-Publication Data
Maxwell, John C.
  How successful people think workbook / John C. Maxwell. — 1st ed.
    p. cm.
  ISBN 978-1-59995-391-5
  1. Success — Psychological aspects.   2. Success — Problems, exercises, etc.
3. Success in business.   4. Creative thinking.   I. Title.
  BF637.S8M34173 2011
  650.1 — dc22

                                                            2010041885

ACKNOWLEDGMENTS

Thank you to

Margaret Maxwell,
who shares her thinking with me daily

Charlie Wetzel,
who writes my books

Stephanie Wetzel,
who assisted in creating this workbook

Linda Eggers,
who runs my life

CONTENTS

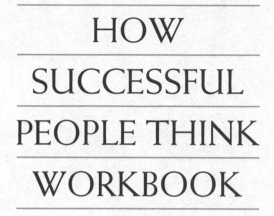

HOW

SUCCESSFUL

PEOPLE THINK

WORKBOOK

INTRODUCTION

Good thinkers are always in demand. A person who knows *how* may always have a job, but the person who knows *why* will always be his boss. Good thinkers solve problems, they never lack ideas that can build an organization, and they always have hope for a better future. Good thinkers rarely find themselves at the mercy of ruthless people who would take advantage of them or try to deceive them, people like Nazi dictator Adolf Hitler, who once boasted, "What luck for rulers that men do not think." Those who develop the process of good thinking can rule themselves—even while under an oppressive ruler or in other difficult circumstances. In short, good thinkers are successful.

I've studied successful people for forty years, and though the diversity you find among them is astounding, I've found that they are all alike in one way: how they think! That is the one thing that separates successful people from unsuccessful ones. And here's the good news: how successful people think can be learned. If you change your thinking, you can change your life!

HOW TO USE THIS WORKBOOK

In my experience, my best thinking has always happened with pen (and yellow legal pad) in hand. Writing down your thoughts and conclusions cements them and makes you more likely to apply them. This workbook is designed not only to teach thinking skills but also as a way to practice them. Some questions will take time—and lots of thought—to answer. Don't rush; instead, take your time and really process your answers. If you don't have enough room to write, start a "Thinking Journal" and process your ideas there. Other sections of this workbook contain action steps. Again, for the lessons in this workbook to have the most impact on your life, it's best to apply what you're learning before you move on.

WHY YOU SHOULD CHANGE YOUR THINKING

It's hard to overstate the value of becoming a good thinker. Good thinking can do many things for you: generate revenue, solve problems, and create opportunities. It can take you to a whole new level—personally and professionally. It really can change your life.

Consider some things you need to know about changing your thinking:

1. Changed Thinking Is Not Automatic

Sadly, a change in thinking doesn't happen on its own. Good ideas rarely go out and find someone. If you want to find a good idea, you must search for it. If you want to become a better thinker, you need to work at it—and once you begin to become a better thinker, the good ideas keep coming. In fact, the amount of good thinking you can do at any time depends primarily on the amount of good thinking you are already doing.

How inclined are you to change? Is a willingness to embrace change evident in your life? Name some areas where you are currently embracing change that shows your openness.

_____

_____

_____

2. Changed Thinking Is Difficult

When you hear someone say, "Now this is just off the top of my head," expect dandruff. The only people who believe thinking is easy are those who don't habitually engage in it. Nobel Prize–winning physicist Albert Einstein, one of the best thinkers who ever lived, asserted, "Thinking is hard work; that's why so few do it." Because thinking is so difficult, you want to use anything you can to help you improve the process.

Have you ever worked with someone who didn't do the hard work of thinking things through? How effective were their decisions and actions as a result? What might have been different if they'd improved their thinking?

_____

_____

_____

3. Changed Thinking Is Worth the Investment

Author Napoleon Hill observed, "More gold has been mined from the thoughts of man than has ever been taken from the earth." When you take the time to learn how to change your thinking and become a better thinker, you are investing in yourself. Gold mines tap out. Stock markets crash. Real estate investments can go sour. But a human mind with the ability to think well is like a diamond mine that never runs out. It's priceless.

What do you want to achieve by becoming a better thinker? What results do you hope to achieve? What are your aspirations?

_____

_____

_____

HOW TO BECOME A BETTER THINKER

Do you want to master the process of good thinking? Do you want to be a better thinker tomorrow than you are today? Then you need to engage in an ongoing process that improves your thinking. Even before you begin to work through the material in each chapter, I recommend that you do the following:

1. Expose Yourself to Good Input

Good thinkers always prime the pump of ideas. They always look for things to get the thinking process started, because what you put in always impacts what comes out.

Read books, review trade magazines, and listen to messages or interviews. And when something you come across intrigues you—whether it's someone else's idea or the seed of an idea that you've come up with yourself—keep it in front of you. Put it in writing and keep it somewhere in your favorite thinking place to stimulate your thinking.

2. Expose Yourself to Good Thinkers

Spend time with the right people. As I worked on this section and bounced my ideas off of some key people (so that my thoughts would be stretched), I realized something about myself. All of the people in my life whom I consider to be close friends or colleagues are thinkers. Now, I love all people. I try to be kind to everyone I meet, and I desire to add value to as many people as I can through conferences, books, audio lessons, etc. But the people I seek out and choose to spend time with all challenge me with their thinking and their actions. They are constantly trying to grow and learn. That's true of my wife, Margaret, my close friends, and the executives who run my companies. Every one of them is a good thinker!

The writer of Proverbs observed that sharp people sharpen one another, just as iron sharpens iron. If you want to be a sharp thinker, be around sharp people.

Who is one of the best thinkers you know who is close to you? Is it a friend, a family member, a colleague? Get in touch with that person and schedule a time to get together. When you meet, ask how he or she became such a good thinker, and what he or she would suggest for you to improve your thinking.

3. Choose to Think Good Thoughts

To become a good thinker, you must become intentional about the thinking process. Regularly put yourself in the right place to think, shape, stretch, and land your thoughts. Make it a priority. Remember, thinking is a discipline.

I asked Dan Cathy, the president of Chick-fil-A, if he made thinking time a high priority. Not only did he say yes, but he told me about what he calls his "thinking schedule." It helps him to fight the hectic pace of life that discourages intentional thinking. Dan says he sets aside time just to think for half a day every two weeks, for one whole day every month, and for two or three full days every year. Dan explains, "This helps me 'keep the main thing the main thing,' since I am so easily distracted."

You may want to do something similar, or you can develop a schedule and method of your own. No matter what you choose to do, go to your thinking place, take paper and pen, and make sure you capture your ideas in writing.

4. Act on Your Good Thoughts

Ideas have a short shelf life. You must act on them before the expiration date. World War I flying ace Eddie Rickenbacker said it all when he remarked, "I can give you a six-word formula for success: Think things through—then follow through."

Have you had a good idea lately but no time to implement it? Don't wait. Think about the first thing you need to do, look at your calendar right now, and schedule time to do it.

5. Allow Your Emotions to Create Another Good Thought

To start the thinking process, you cannot rely on your feelings. In *Failing Forward,* I wrote that you can act your way into feeling long before you can feel your way into action. If you wait until you feel like doing something, you will likely never accomplish it. The same is true for thinking. You cannot wait until you *feel* like thinking. However, I've found that once you engage in the process of good thinking, you can use your emotions to feed the process and create mental momentum.

Try it for yourself. After you go through the disciplined process of thinking and enjoy some success, allow yourself to savor the moment and try riding the mental energy of that success. If you're like me, it's likely to spur additional thoughts and productive ideas.

6. Repeat the Process

One good thought does not make a good life. The people who have one good thought and try to ride it for an entire career often end up unhappy or destitute. They are the one-hit wonders, the one-book authors, the one-message speakers, the one-time inventors who spend their life struggling to protect or promote their single idea. Success comes to those who have an entire mountain of gold that they continually mine, not those who find one nugget and try to live on it for fifty years. To become someone who can mine a lot of gold, you need to keep repeating the process of good thinking.

Think about your daily routine. When can you regularly schedule thinking time?

PUTTING YOURSELF IN THE RIGHT PLACE TO THINK

Becoming a good thinker isn't overly complicated. It's a discipline. If you do the six things I have outlined above, you will set yourself up for a lifestyle of better thinking. But what do you do to come up with specific ideas on a day-to-day basis?

I want to teach you the process that I've used to discover and develop good thoughts. It's certainly not the only one that works, but it has worked well for me.

1. Find a Place to Think Your Thoughts

If you go to your designated place to think expecting to generate good thoughts, then eventually you will come up with some. Where is the best place to think? Everybody's different. Some people think best in the shower. Others, like my friend Dick Biggs, like to go to a park. For me, the best places to think are in my car, on planes, and in the pool. Ideas come to me in other places as well, such as when

I'm in bed. (I keep a special lighted writing pad on my nightstand for such times.) I believe I often get thoughts because I make it a habit to frequently go to my thinking places.

If you want to consistently generate ideas, you need to do the same thing. Find a place where you can think, and plan to capture your thoughts on paper so that you don't lose them. When I found a place to think my thoughts, my thoughts found a place in me.

Identify a place you have regular, easy access to that you can designate as your thinking place. Stock it with whatever tools and resources you need to be able to think while there.

2. Find a Place to Shape Your Thoughts

Rarely do ideas come fully formed and completely worked out. Most of the time, they need to be shaped until they have substance. As my friend Dan Reiland says, they have to "stand the test of clarity and questioning." During the shaping time, you want to hold an idea up to strong scrutiny. Many times a thought that seemed outstanding late at night looks pretty silly in the light of day.

Ask questions about your ideas. Fine-tune them. One of the best ways to do that is to put your thoughts in writing. Professor, college president, and U.S. senator S. I. Hayakawa wrote, "Learning to write is learning to think. You don't know anything clearly unless you can state it in writing."

As you shape your thoughts, you find out whether an idea has potential. You learn what you have. You also learn some things about yourself. The shaping time thrills me because it embodies:

- **Humor:** The thoughts that don't work often provide comic relief.
- **Humility:** The moments when I connect with God awe me.
- **Excitement:** I love to play out an idea mentally (what I call "futuring" it).
- **Creativity:** In these moments I am unhampered by reality.
- **Fulfillment:** God made me for this process; it uses my greatest gifts and gives me joy.
- **Honesty:** As I turn over an idea in my mind, I discover my true motives.

- **Passion:** When you shape a thought, you find out what you believe and what really counts.
- **Change:** Most of the changes I have made in my life resulted from thorough thinking on a subject.

You can shape your thoughts almost anywhere. Just find a place that works for you, where you will be able to write things down, focus your attention without interruptions, and ask questions about your ideas.

3. Find a Place to Stretch Your Thoughts

If you come upon great thoughts and spend time mentally shaping them, don't think you're done and can stop there. If you do, you will miss some of the most valuable aspects of the thinking process. You miss bringing others in and expanding ideas to their greatest potential.

Earlier in my life, I have to admit, I was often guilty of this error. I wanted to take an idea from seed thought to solution before sharing it with anyone, even the people it would most impact. I did this both at work and at home. But over the years, I have learned that you can go much further with a team than you can go alone.

I've found a kind of formula that can help you stretch your thoughts. It says,

The Right **Thought** plus the Right **People**

in the Right **Environment** at the Right **Time**

for the Right **Reason** = the **Right Result**

This combination is hard to beat. Like every person, every thought has the potential to become something great. When you find a place to stretch your thoughts, you find that potential.

Identify the key people in your life with whom you will interact to stretch your thoughts. Some people may help you in all aspects of your life. Others may work with you in only a specific area.

4. Find a Place to Land Your Thoughts

Author C. D. Jackson observes that "great ideas need landing gear as well as wings." Any idea that remains only an idea doesn't make a great impact. The real power of an idea comes when it goes from abstraction to application. Think about Einstein's theory of relativity. When he published his theories in 1905 and 1916, they were merely profound ideas. Their real power came with the development of the nuclear reactor in 1942 and the nuclear bomb in 1945. When scientists developed and implemented Einstein's ideas, the whole world changed.

Likewise, if you want your thoughts to make an impact, you need to land them with others so that they can someday be implemented. As you plan for the application phase of the thinking process, land your ideas first with:

- **Yourself:** Landing an idea with yourself will give you integrity. People will buy into an idea only after they buy into the leader who communicates it. Before teaching any lesson, I ask myself three questions: *Do I believe it? Do I live it? Do I believe others should live it?* If I can't answer yes to all three questions, then I haven't landed it.
- **Key Players:** Let's face it, no idea will fly if the influencers don't embrace it. After all, they are the people who carry thoughts from idea to implementation.
- **Those Most Affected:** Landing thoughts with the people on the firing line will give you great insight. Those closest to changes that occur as a result of a new idea can give you a "reality read." And that's important, because sometimes even when you've diligently completed the process of creating a thought, shaping it, and stretching it with other good thinkers, you can still miss the mark.

Have you had an idea lately of how something could be improved? Fill in the worksheet below about that idea.

Idea:

_____

Do I believe it?

_____

Do l live it?

_____

Do I believe others should live it?

_____

Whom do I need to carry out this idea? Who are the key players?

_____

_____

Who is most affected by this idea?

_____

5. Find a Place to Fly Your Thoughts

French philosopher Henri-Louis Bergson, who won the Nobel Prize in literature in 1927, asserted that a person should "think like a man of action, act like a man of thought." What good is thinking if it has no application in real life? Thinking divorced from actions cannot be productive. Learning how to master the process of thinking well leads you to productive thinking. If you can develop the discipline of good thinking and turn it into a lifetime habit, then you will be successful and productive all of your life. Once you've created, shaped, stretched, and landed your thoughts, then flying them can be fun and easy.

When it comes to generating ideas and putting them into practice, which is the greater strength for you? What must you do to improve the weaker of the two?

_____

_____

_____

PORTRAIT OF A GOOD THINKER

You often hear someone say that a colleague or friend is a "good thinker," but that phrase means something different to everyone. To one person it may mean having a high IQ, while to another it could mean knowing a bunch of trivia or being able to figure out "who done it" when reading a mystery novel. I believe that good thinking isn't just one thing. It consists of several specific thinking skills. Becoming a good thinker means developing those skills to the best of your ability.

It doesn't matter whether you were born rich or poor. It doesn't matter if you have a third-grade education or possess a PhD. It doesn't matter if you suffer from multiple disabilities or you're the picture of health. No matter what your circumstances, you can learn to be a good thinker. All you must do is be willing to engage in the process every day.

In *Built to Last,* Jim Collins and Jerry Porras describe what it means to be a visionary company, the kind of company that epitomizes the pinnacle of American business:

> A visionary company is like a great work of art. Think of Michelangelo's scenes from Genesis on the ceiling of the Sistine Chapel or his statue of David. Think of a great and enduring novel, like *Huckleberry Finn* or *Crime and Punishment.* Think of Beethoven's Ninth Symphony or Shakespeare's *Henry V.* Think of a beautifully designed building, like the masterpieces of Frank Lloyd Wright or Ludwig Mies van der Rohe. You can't point to any one single item that makes the whole thing work; it's the *entire* work — all the pieces working together to create an overall effect — that leads to enduring greatness.[1]

Good thinking is similar. You need all the thinking "pieces" to become the kind of person who can achieve great things. Those pieces include the following eleven skills:

- Seeing the Wisdom of Big-Picture Thinking
- Unleashing the Potential of Focused Thinking
- Discovering the Joy of Creative Thinking
- Recognizing the Importance of Realistic Thinking
- Releasing the Power of Strategic Thinking
- Feeling the Energy of Possibility Thinking
- Embracing the Lessons of Reflective Thinking

- Questioning the Acceptance of Popular Thinking
- Encouraging the Participation of Shared Thinking
- Experiencing the Satisfaction of Unselfish Thinking
- Enjoying the Return of Bottom-Line Thinking

As you read the chapters dedicated to each kind of thinking and work through the questions, you will discover I do not try to tell you *what* to think; my goal is to teach you *how* to think. As you become acquainted with each skill, you will find that some you do well, others you don't. Learn to develop each kind of thinking, and you will become a better thinker. Master all that you can—including the process of shared thinking, which helps you compensate for your weak areas—and your life will change.

WHAT KIND OF THINKER ARE YOU?

Write a plus sign next to the following words that you feel best describe you, and a minus sign next to those that you feel are least like you. Be as honest with yourself as possible.

☐ Altruistic (10)   ☐ Generous (10)   ☐ Pensive (7)
☐ Approachable (9)   ☐ Goal oriented (2) ☐ Planner (5)
☐ Artistic (3)   ☐ Innovative (8)   ☐ Practical (4)
☐ Brainstormer (3)   ☐ Inquisitive (6)   ☐ Restrained (4)
☐ Broad-minded (1) ☐ Intentional (2)   ☐ Results oriented (11)
☐ Cautious (7)   ☐ Minimalistic (11) ☐ Risk averse (4)
☐ Collaborative (9)   ☐ Observant (7)   ☐ Selective (2)
☐ Direct (11)   ☐ Optimistic (6)   ☐ Structured (5)
☐ Expansive (1)   ☐ Organized (5)   ☐ Thoughtful (10)
☐ Experimental (8)   ☐ Original (8)   ☐ Tolerant (1)
☐ Extrovert (9)   ☐ Out of the box (3) ☐ Visionary (6)

Take a look at the numbers next to the adjectives. Those numbers correspond to the different types of thinking and the chapter numbers in this book. If you have pluses next to the 3s, you're probably a strong creative thinker. If you had minuses next to the 5s, you'll want to spend extra time on chapter 5 to improve your strategic thinking. If you placed neither a plus nor a minus next to certain numbers, those numbers represent areas where you probably feel you are average and could perhaps improve in. Even for the areas in which you are strong, you will still want to work through those chapters to become even stronger.

1: Big-Picture Thinker

2: Focused Thinker

3: Creative Thinker

4: Realistic Thinker

5: Strategic Thinker

6: Possibility Thinker

7: Reflective Thinker

8: Unpopular Thinker

9: Shared Thinker

10: Unselfish Thinker

11: Bottom-Line Thinker

DISCUSSION QUESTIONS

1. How would you describe or define a good thinker?
2. Name some of your favorite thinkers from history. What makes you admire them?
3. Who is the best thinker in your field? Explain. Do most people in your field agree with your assessment? If not, why do you think this person is the best?
4. In your personal experience with education, did your teachers and their methods place high value on thinking skills?
5. How would you define success?
6. How does good thinking come into play when it comes to success?
7. Do you agree that most successful people tend to think in the same ways? Why?
8. What do you hope to gain from working through this book? In what areas are you skeptical? What would it take for you to embrace the idea of good thinking improving your chances for success?

Cultivate Big-Picture Thinking

Where success is concerned, people are not measured in inches or pounds or college degrees, or family background; they are measured by the size of their thinking.

— DAVID SCHWARTZ

Writer Henry David Thoreau wrote, "Many an object is not seen, though it falls within the range of our *visual* ray, because it does not come within the range of our *intellectual* ray" (emphasis mine). Human beings are in the habit of seeing their own world first. However, big-picture thinkers realize there is a world out there besides their own, and they make an effort to get outside of themselves and see other people's worlds through their eyes. It's hard to see the picture when you're inside the frame.

French essayist Michel Eyquem de Montaigne wrote, "The value of life lies not in the length of days, but in the use we make of them; a man may live long yet live very little." Becoming a big-picture thinker can help you to live with wholeness, to live a very fulfilling life. People who see the big picture expand their experience because they expand their world. As a result, they are able to accomplish more than narrow-minded people. And they experience fewer unwanted surprises, too, because in any given situation they are more likely to see the many components involved: issues, people, relationships, timing, and values. They are also, therefore, usually more tolerant of other people and their thinking.

BIG-PICTURE THINKING CASE STUDY

An Egyptian librarian heard that the sun could be seen shining at the bottom of a well in the town of Syene on the longest day of the year. He was a big-picture thinker, so it started him thinking. He surmised that if it made a reflection in a well, the sun must be directly overhead. And if the sun were directly overhead, then it would cast no shadows from upright columns or posts. Yet on the longest day of the year in the city of Alexandria, where he lived, he observed that straight columns did cast shadows.

He decided to travel the eight hundred kilometers to Syene himself to verify that what he had heard was true. On the longest day of the year, he looked into the well and saw the sun reflected. And sure enough, at midday, posts in Syene cast no shadows.

He reflected on that. After a while, he began to see a bigger picture of what these seemingly unconnected facts meant. Surprisingly, it went against what nearly everyone believed at the time. You see, the librarian's name was Eratosthenes, and he lived more than twenty-two hundred years ago.

As the director of the greatest library in the world (the library of Alexandria in Egypt was said to possess hundreds of thousands of scrolls), Eratosthenes was at the intellectual capital of the world for his time. In the third century BC, nearly every scholar in Alexandria and around the world believed that the earth was flat. But Eratosthenes reasoned that if the sun's light came down straight and the earth was flat, then there would be no shadows in both Alexandria and Syene. If there were shadows in one location but not the other, then there could be only one logical explanation. The surface of the earth must be curved. In other words, the world must be a sphere.

That was a pretty impressive mental leap, although it seems perfectly logical to us today. After all, we've seen pictures of our planet from space. But Eratosthenes made that big-picture connection by using everyday facts and putting them together. What's even more impressive is that he took it a step further. He actually calculated the size of the earth! Using basic trigonometry, he measured the angle of the shadows and calculated that it was approximately 7.12 degrees. That's about one-fiftieth of a circle. And he reasoned that if the distance between Syene (modern-day Aswan) and Alexandria was 800 kilometers, then the earth must be around 40,000 kilometers in circumference (50 × 800 kilometers). He wasn't far off; the actual circumference of the earth through the poles is 40,008 kilometers. Not bad for a guy who had nothing but his brain and a big-picture mind-set to figure the whole thing out!

APPLYING THE CASE STUDY

In the actions of Eratosthenes, you can see the truth of a statement made many centuries later by German statesman Konrad Adenauer: "We all live under the same sky, but we don't all have the same horizon." As you consider the story of the librarian of Alexandria, answer these questions:

1. Why do you think Eratosthenes was able to make the connection about the earth while thousands of others missed it? What qualities do you think big-picture thinkers usually possess? List them here.

   _____

   _____

   _____

2. Who in your personal acquaintance best exemplifies big-picture thinking? What has this person done to cultivate it? Do you think his or her ability is a function of experience, vision, education, training, temperament, or something else?

   _____

   _____

   _____

3. Do you see any similarities between the big-picture thinker you know personally and Eratosthenes? Explain.

   _____

   _____

   _____

4. Who in your acquaintance seems to be incapable of big-picture thinking? What is that person's background, education, training, and temperament? If you were to compare this person to the big-picture thinker you know, how would you describe their differences? What can you learn from the contrast between the two?

   _____

   _____

   _____

HOW BIG-PICTURE THINKING CAN
MAKE YOU MORE SUCCESSFUL

The most successful people in life focus on and work within their strengths, and many of them are fairly narrow when it comes to talent and abilities. However, there are very few successful people who lack the ability to see the big picture. It's very difficult for someone who loses perspective to be successful because one needs to see the big picture in order to make good decisions. In addition, the ability to see the big picture also has several specific benefits:

1. Big-Picture Thinking Allows You to Lead

You can find many big-picture thinkers who aren't leaders, but you will find few leaders who are not big-picture thinkers. Leaders must be able to do many important things for their people:

- **See the vision before their people do.** They also see more of it. This allows them to...
- **Size up situations, taking into account many variables.** Leaders who see the big picture discern possibilities as well as problems and can then form a foundation to build the vision. Once leaders have done that, they can...
- **Sketch a picture of where the team is going,** including any potential challenges or obstacles. The goal of leaders shouldn't be merely to make their people feel good, but to help them be good and accomplish the dream. The vision, shown accurately, will allow leaders to...
- **Show how the future connects with the past to make the journey more meaningful.** When leaders recognize this need for connection and bridge it, then they can...
- **Seize the moment when the timing is right.** In leadership, when you move is as important as what you do. As Winston Churchill said, "There comes a special moment in everyone's life, a moment for which that person was born.... When he seizes it...it is his finest hour."

Leaders who are constantly looking at the whole picture have the best chance of succeeding in any endeavor.

Where do you typically fit when it comes to vision in an organization?

- ☐ *Visionary—the person who senses or develops the vision for the organization*
- ☐ *Vision Carrier—someone who helps communicate the vision to the organization*
- ☐ *Early Adopter—someone who receives the vision and immediately embraces it*
- ☐ *Middle Adopter—someone who needs time to understand and accept the vision*
- ☐ *Late Adopter—someone who needs the validity of the vision proven before adapting*
- ☐ *Critic—someone who would rather fight than follow*

If you are a middle adopter, late adopter, or critic, you need to work on your ability to see the big picture.

2. Big-Picture Thinking Keeps You on Target

Thomas Fuller, chaplain to Charles II of England, observed, "He that is everywhere is nowhere." To get things done, you need focus. However, to get the right things done, you also need to consider the big picture. Only by putting your daily activities in the context of the big picture will you be able to stay on target. As Alvin Toffler says, "You've got to think about big things while you're doing small things, so that all the small things go in the right direction."

What process do you have in place in your life to keep you focused? Do you have a constant touchstone or reference point that you can use to make sure you are doing the right things and not just keeping busy with unimportant activity?

_____

_____

_____

Some people use core values, a mission statement, a set of goals, or a picture to help them remember the big picture. What can you use?

_____

_____

_____

3. Big-Picture Thinking Allows You to See What Others See

One of the most important skills you can develop in human relations is the ability to see things from the other person's point of view. It's one of the keys to working with clients, satisfying customers, maintaining a marriage, rearing children, helping those who are less fortunate, etc. All human interactions are enhanced by the ability to put yourself in another person's shoes.

How good are you at seeing things from others' perspective. Rate yourself on a scale of 1 to 10.

1 2 3 4 5 6 7 8 9 10

Now ask three trusted friends, family members, or colleagues to rate you by the same scale.

Name   **Rating**

_____   1 2 3 4 5 6 7 8 9 10

_____   1 2 3 4 5 6 7 8 9 10

_____   1 2 3 4 5 6 7 8 9 10

If their numbers and yours differ by more than one, then your self-perception is off. If your numbers are lower than 6, this is an area where you need to work to improve.

4. Big-Picture Thinking Promotes Teamwork

If you participate in any kind of team activity, then you know how important it is that team members see the whole picture, not just their own part. When a person doesn't know how his work fits with that of his teammates, then the whole team is in trouble. The better the grasp team members have of the big picture, the greater their potential to work together as a team.

In your profession, how does your role fit in with the larger purpose of the organization? How does it fit in your industry? Why are the other people who are part of the process also important? (If you can't describe their importance—or, worse yet, you fail to see it—then your lack of big-picture thinking will limit your professional progress.)

_____

_____

_____

5. Big-Picture Thinking Keeps You from Being Caught Up in the Mundane

Let's face it: some aspects of everyday life are absolutely necessary but thoroughly uninteresting. Big-picture thinkers don't let the grind get to them, because they don't lose sight of the all-important overview. They know that the person who forgets the ultimate is a slave to the immediate.

Do mundane activities that you must accomplish get you down? How can you use big-picture thinking and a sense of purpose or mission to keep you from becoming discouraged?

_____

_____

_____

6. Big-Picture Thinking Helps You to Chart Uncharted Territory

Have you ever heard the expression, "We'll cross that bridge when we come to it"? That phrase undoubtedly was coined by someone who had trouble seeing the big picture. The world was built by people who "crossed bridges" in their minds long before anyone else did. The only way to break new ground or move into uncharted territory is to look beyond the immediate and see the big picture.

How much time do you spend thinking about future goals, innovative ideas, new methods of doing things, improving the organization, and the like? Do you believe that is your responsibility, or have you allowed others to assume that role? Why? How can you use big-picture thinking to help you focus on taking new territory professionally?

_____

_____

_____

WHAT IF YOU BECAME BETTER AT
BIG-PICTURE THINKING?

We can only change, grow, and improve in areas where we acknowledge that we need to improve. Think very honestly about yourself when it comes to big-picture thinking. How much do you need to improve in this area? What might change in your life if you were to start thinking from a big-picture perspective? How would that impact you professionally? Relationally? Financially? Spiritually? Spend some time reflecting and recording your thoughts here.

_____

_____

_____

_____

_____

_____

_____

_____

_____

_____

_____

_____

_____

_____

_____

_____

_____

_____

_____

HOW TO BECOME A BIG-PICTURE THINKER

If you desire to seize new opportunities and open new horizons, then you need to add big-picture thinking to your abilities. People do not become successful without that ability. To become a good thinker better able to see the big picture, keep in mind the following:

1. Don't Strive for Certainty

Big-picture thinkers are comfortable with ambiguity. They don't try to force every observation or piece of data into preformulated mental cubbyholes. They think broadly and can juggle many seemingly contradictory thoughts in their minds. If you want to cultivate the ability to think big picture, then you must get used to embracing and dealing with complex and diverse ideas.

2. Learn from Every Experience

Big-picture thinkers broaden their outlook by striving to learn from every experience. They don't rest on their successes, they learn from them. More important, they learn from their failures. They can do that because they remain teachable.

Varied experiences — both positive and negative — help you see the big picture. The greater the variety of experience and success you have, the more potential to learn. If you desire to be a big-picture thinker, then get out there and try a lot of things, take a lot of chances, and take time to learn after every victory or defeat.

3. Gain Insight from a Variety of People

Big-picture thinkers learn from their experiences. But they also learn from experiences they don't have. That is, they learn by receiving insight from others — from customers, employees, colleagues, and leaders.

If you desire to broaden your thinking and see more of the big picture, then seek out mentors and counselors to help you. But be wise in whom you ask for advice. Gaining insight from a variety of people doesn't mean stopping anyone and everyone in hallways and grocery store lines and asking what they think about a given subject. Be selective. Talk to people who know and care about you, who know their field, and who bring experience deeper and broader than your own.

4. Give Yourself Permission to Expand Your World

If you want to be a big-picture thinker, you will have to go against the flow of the world. Society wants to keep people in boxes. Most people are married mentally to the status quo. They want what was, not what can be. They seek safety and simple answers. To think big picture, you need to give yourself permission to go a different way, to break new ground, to find new worlds to conquer. And when your world does get bigger, you need to celebrate. Never forget there is more out there in the world than what you've experienced.

Keep learning, keep growing, and keep looking at the big picture! If you desire to be a good thinker, that's what you need to do.

BIG-PICTURE THINKING ACTION PLAN

1. **Revisit the Vision:** Good big-picture thinkers rarely lose sight of the vision and overall picture, and for that reason they don't get caught up in too many details or side issues. So take some time to clarify the vision of your area of responsibility, your organization, and your industry or field. Take time to clarify the vision for your life and for your family.

   If you've spent time in the past discovering these things, then revisit them. Reflect on them. Write them out. Put the written vision, or something that symbolizes it, someplace where you will see it every day so that you don't lose sight of it.

   If you've never clarified these issues, spend your time discovering and articulating them. Then keep them in front of you.

2. **Broaden Your Experience:** Big-picture thinkers bring into play knowledge from a variety of areas. How can you broaden yours? Pick something to learn this year that takes you out of your comfort zone and gives you experiences far different from anything you've done before. If it turns out to be something you really enjoy and benefit from, continue in it after a year. If not, pick something new and give it a year. In ten years, you should have such a broad range of experience that you add value to your organization in terms of your perspective.

3. **Gain Insight from Others:** Find a mentor in your field whose experience and wisdom exceeds yours, and ask to meet with him or her on a regular basis. However long the meeting is, spend three to five times as much time preparing beforehand. In other words, if you will meet for an hour, spend three to five hours preparing: do research to know the person's strengths, carefully consider what questions to ask, etc. And after you meet, create an action plan to implement what you've learned. Also, be sure the next time you meet to explain how you've applied what you were told during the previous meeting.

4. **Integrate the Parts of Your World:** Most industries or professions require various skill sets, departments, or factions to work together. For example, for someone to be successful as a state representative, he or she would need to understand not only how to campaign for office and fulfill the duties of the office, but also how the house of representatives interacts with the state senate, the executive branch, and the judiciary.

Take some time to learn how all of the various departments or functions in your field interact with one another, how they function when working well together, where the hang-ups and pitfalls lie, etc. Expertise informs big-picture thinking.

AN EXERCISE IN BIG-PICTURE THINKING

Thinking with the big picture in mind often means seeing situations from an entirely different perspective. Conflict is a great training ground for this.

1. Name one conflict that you either witnessed or took part in recently.

   _____

   _____

   _____

2. Argue for the side that you *disagree* with, listing three valid reasons for their perspective and beliefs.

   a. _____

   _____

   b. _____

   _____

   c. _____

   _____

3. Pretend that you *do* agree with that side of the argument. What life experiences, priorities, and values would cause you to believe the way you do?

DISCUSSION QUESTIONS

1. Do you identify with the story of Eratosthenes, or was it too different from your own life experience? What might have been a better case study?
2. Do you think a person can be successful without practicing big-picture thinking? Explain.
3. What role does big-picture thinking play in leadership?
4. In what areas of your life do you practice big-picture thinking effectively? In what areas do you sometimes find it a challenge?
5. What do you find to be the greatest challenge or obstacle to big-picture thinking?
6. If you become better at big-picture thinking, what impact will it have on your life?
7. What must you do to become a better big-picture thinker? How must you change?
8. Do you intend to implement any of the suggestions in the action plan? If so, which ones? If not, what actions would you consider more helpful? How will you implement them?

2

Engage in Focused Thinking

He did each thing as if he did nothing else.
— SPOKEN OF NOVELIST CHARLES DICKENS

Sociologist Robert Lynd observed that "knowledge is power only if man knows what facts not to bother with." Focused thinking removes distractions and mental clutter so that you can concentrate on an issue and think with clarity.

No matter whether your goal is to increase your level of play, sharpen your business plan, improve your bottom line, develop your subordinates, or solve personal problems, you need to focus. Of course, it's not always easy; you can't focus on everything that you might like to. But the earlier you learn to give up some things in order to focus on what has the greatest impact, the sooner you can dedicate yourself to excellence in what matters most.

FOCUSED THINKING CASE STUDY

Most people spend lots of time drawing and coloring with crayons when they are kids. One source says that children in the United States will, on average, wear down 730 crayons by the time they are ten years old. That's a lot of creative energy! Think back to your childhood. Can you picture the kind of crayons you used? In your mind you can probably picture the crayons and even the shape and color of the box—a yellow box with green letters. You can probably even imagine what they smell like. And what's the brand name on that box? In all likelihood, it's Crayola.

After all, Crayola is the most popular and recognized brand of crayons in the world. Every year, Binney & Smith, the company that makes Crayola products, manufactures nearly three billion crayons at a rate of twelve million a day. That's enough crayons to circle the globe six times!

The company was founded by Joseph Binney in 1864 as the Peekskill Chemical Works. In 1885, the founder's son, Edwin, and his cousin, C. Harold Smith, became partners and changed the company's name to Binney & Smith. Up to the turn of the century, the company's main products were items such as red pigments for barn paint and carbon black used in making lampblack or automobile tires. Their primary method of product development was simple: ask their customers what their needs were and then develop products in the laboratory to meet those needs.

In 1900, the company began making slate pencils for the educational market, and they found that teachers were happy to tell company representatives what they desired. When teachers complained about poor chalk, Binney & Smith produced a superior, dustless variety. When teachers complained that they couldn't buy a decent American crayon (the best were imported from Europe and very expensive), the company developed the Crayola. The product was introduced to the market in 1903 as a box of eight colors that cost a nickel.

Once they found their niche in the children's market, Crayola became incredibly focused. For more than a hundred years, they have manufactured superior art supplies for children. Today they dominate that market—even in the face of the electronic revolution.

In *The Five Faces of Genius,* Annette Moser-Wellman assessed the company by saying,

> The biggest threat to Crayola's business has been the entry of computer games for kids. Instead of drawing and coloring, kids are tempted by interactive CDs and more. Instead of trying to dominate computer games, Crayola has chosen to flourish within their limitations. They do children's art products better than anyone.[1]

Binney & Smith could have lost focus in an attempt to chase new markets and diversify themselves. That was what toy manufacturer Coleco did. The company started out in leather goods in the 1950s and then switched to plastics. In the late 1960s, they were the world's largest manufacturer of aboveground swimming pools. They had found their niche. Yet in the 1970s and 1980s, they chased after the computer game market and then low-end computers. (You may remember ColecoVision.) Then they tried to capitalize on Cabbage Patch dolls. It ultimately drove them into bankruptcy.

It would have been easy for Binney & Smith to chase after other successes, but they didn't do that. The company has remained focused. And as long as it does, it will continue to excel and to sell more crayons and children's art supplies than any other company in the world.

APPLYING THE CASE STUDY

Spend some time thinking about Binney & Smith's story and answer the following questions:

1. On the surface, listening to all the needs of your customers could appear to make a company *less* focused rather than *more* focused. How does one know what information to take to heart and what to dismiss?

   _____

   _____

   _____

2. At some point the leaders at Binney & Smith had to decide to narrow their focus and concentrate on a particular group of products. What criteria do you think they used? What criteria do you use in your own field or profession?

   _____

   _____

   _____

3. What differences do you see in the way Binney & Smith and Coleco approached innovation? What made one successful while the other floundered?

   _____

   _____

   _____

4. Based on your knowledge of Crayola products, how focused do you think they have remained? How has that impacted their effectiveness? (If your knowledge is limited, then visit a store or website that sells children's art supplies.)

   _____

   _____

   _____

5. How focused are you in your profession or industry? How has it impacted your effectiveness?

_____

_____

_____

HOW FOCUSED THINKING CAN
MAKE YOU MORE SUCCESSFUL

Just as focus is important in developing products for a company, it is also important in developing ideas for an individual. Focused thinking can do several things for you:

1. Focused Thinking Harnesses Energy Toward a Desired Goal

In his book *Focus: The Future of Your Company Depends on It,* marketing consultant Al Ries gives a tremendous illustration:

> The sun is a powerful source of energy. Every hour the sun washes the earth with billions of kilowatts of energy. Yet with a hat and some sunscreen you can bathe in the light of the sun for hours at a time with few ill effects.
>
> A laser is a weak source of energy. A laser takes a few watts of energy and focuses them in a coherent stream of light. But with a laser you can drill a hole in a diamond or wipe out a cancer.[2]

Focus can bring energy and power to almost anything, whether it's physical or mental. If you're learning how to pitch a baseball and you want to develop a good curveball, then focused thinking while practicing will improve your technique. If you need to refine the manufacturing process of your product, focused thinking will help you develop the best method. If you want to solve a difficult mathematics problem, sustaining focused thinking helps you break through to the solution. Philosopher Bertrand Russell asserted, "To be able to concentrate for a considerable time is essential to difficult achievement." The greater the difficulty of a problem or issue, the more focused-thinking time will be necessary to solve it.

How effective are you typically when it comes to focused thinking? Is it generally a strength or a weakness for you? Why?

_____

_____

_____

2. Focused Thinking Gives Ideas Time to Develop

One of my favorite things to do is to surface and develop ideas. I often bring my creative team together for brainstorming and creative thinking. When we first get together, we try to be exhaustive in our thinking in order to generate as many ideas as possible. That has great value because the birthing of a potential breakthrough is often the result of sharing a lot of good ideas.

But to take ideas to the next level, you need to shift from being expansive in your thinking to being selective. Over the years, I have discovered that a good idea can become a great idea when it is given focus time. It's true that focusing on an idea for a long time can be very frustrating. I've often spent days focusing on a thought and trying to develop it, only to find that I could not improve the idea. But sometimes my perseverance in focused thinking pays off. That brings me great joy. And when focused thinking is at its best, not only does the idea grow, but so do I!

How much time do you dedicate to focused thinking on a regular basis—daily or weekly?

_____

_____

_____

3. Focused Thinking Brings Clarity to the Target

Focused thinking removes distractions and mental clutter so that you can concentrate on an issue and think with clarity. That's crucial, because if you don't know what the target is, how will you ever hit it?

A favorite hobby of mine is playing golf. It's a wonderfully challenging game. I like it because the objectives are so clear. Professor William Mobley of the University of South Carolina made the following observation about golf:

One of the most important things about golf is the presence of clear goals. You see the pins, you know the par—it's neither too easy nor unattainable, you know your average score, and there are competitive goals — competitive with par, with yourself and others. These goals give you something to shoot at. In work, as in golf, goals motivate.

One time on the golf course, I followed a golfer who neglected to put the pin back in the hole after he putted. Because I could not see my target, I couldn't focus properly. My focus quickly turned to frustration — and to poor play. Because my target was unclear, my focus was diminished. To be a good golfer, a person needs to focus. The same is true in thinking. Focus helps you to know the goal — and to achieve it.

The ability to focus often depends on knowing yourself and what you need. What helps you to become more focused — what conditions, what activities? What inhibits your ability to think with focus?

_____

_____

_____

4. Focused Thinking Will Take You to the Next Level

No one achieves greatness by becoming a generalist. You don't hone a skill by diluting your attention to its development. The only way to get to the next level is to focus. No matter whether your goal is to increase your level of play, sharpen your business plan, improve your bottom line, develop your subordinates, or solve personal problems, you need to focus. Author Harry A. Overstreet observed, "The immature mind hops from one thing to another; the mature mind seeks to follow through."

In *The Road Less Traveled,* M. Scott Peck includes a telling story about himself and his personal ineptitude when it came to fixing things. He said that anytime he attempted to make minor repairs or put anything together, the result was always confusion, failure, and frustration. Then one day on a walk, he saw a neighbor repairing a lawn mower. Peck told the man, "Boy, I sure admire you. I've never been able to fix those kind of things or do anything like that."

"That's because you don't take the time," the neighbor answered. After reflecting on the man's statement, Peck decided to test whether it was true. The next time he was faced with a mechanical challenge, he took his time and focused his attention on the problem. Much to his surprise, at age thirty-seven, he was finally able to succeed.

After that, he says that he knew that he was not "cursed or genetically defective or otherwise incapacitated or impotent." If he wanted to go to the next level in that area of his life, he could do it if he was willing to focus on it. But instead, he now makes a conscious choice to focus his attention on his profession: psychiatry.[3]

What area of your life is in the greatest need of your focused thinking? Why?

_____

_____

_____

WHAT IF YOU BECAME BETTER AT
FOCUSED THINKING?

We can only change, grow, and improve in areas where we acknowledge that we need to improve. Think very honestly about yourself when it comes to focused thinking. How much do you need to improve in this area? What might change in your life if you were to start thinking in a more focused way? How would that impact you professionally? Relationally? Financially? Spiritually? Spend some time reflecting and recording your thoughts here.

HOW TO BECOME A FOCUSED THINKER

Does every area of your life deserve dedicated, focused thinking time? Of course, the answer is no. Be selective, not exhaustive, in your focused thinking. And once you have a handle on what you should think about, you must decide how to better focus on it. Here are five suggestions to help you with the process:

1. Remove Distractions

I've found that I need blocks of time to think without interruption. So when necessary, I make myself unavailable and go off to my "thinking place." As a leader, however, I am aware that I need to remain accessible to others *and* to withdraw from them to think.

But since one lets us connect with people and know their needs, and the other lets us think of ways to add value to them, we need to value and give attention to both.

2. Make Time for Focused Thinking

Once you have a place to think, you need the time to think. Years ago I realized that my best thinking time occurs in the morning. So whenever possible, I reserve my mornings for thinking and writing. One way to gain time for focused thinking is to impose upon yourself a rule that one company implemented. Don't allow yourself to look at e-mail until after 10 a.m. Instead, focus your energies on your number one priority. Put time wasters on hold so that you can create thinking time for yourself.

3. Keep Items of Focus Before You

Ralph Waldo Emerson, the great transcendental thinker, believed, "Concentration is the secret of strength in politics, in war, in trade, in short, in all management of human affairs." To benefit from that concentration, keep important items in front of you. Ask a colleague or assistant to keep bringing them up. Or keep a file or a page where you see it every day as you work. That strategy has successfully helped me for thirty years to stimulate and sharpen ideas.

4. Set Goals

I believe goals are important. The mind will not focus until it has clear objectives. But the purpose of goals is to focus your attention and give you direction, not to identify a final destination. As you think about your goals, note that they should be

- Clear enough to be kept in focus
- Close enough to be achieved
- Helpful enough to change lives

Be sure to write down your goals. And if you *really* want to make sure they're focused, take the advice of David Belasco, who says, "If you can't write your idea on the back of my business card, you don't have a clear idea."

5. Question Your Progress

Ask yourself, "Am I seeing a return for my investment of focused thinking time? Is what I am doing getting me closer to my goals? Am I headed in a direction that helps me to fulfill my commitments, maintain my priorities, and realize my dreams?"

FOCUSED THINKING ACTION PLAN

1. **Set Aside Dedicated Thinking Time:** You will not have focused thinking time unless you intentionally create it. Using your calendar, set aside a block of time every day for thinking. Ideally, it should fall in your most productive time of day. Schedule it and then protect it as you would any other important appointment.

2. **Create Space for Focused Thinking:** One of the greatest enemies of focused thinking is distraction. Create an environment for good thinking. Find a place where you won't be interrupted, distracted, or tempted — by people, your phone, the computer, social media, television, etc. (Yes, it is possible! But you may have to fight for it.) Then spend your scheduled time in that setting. Stick with it. It may take you many sessions before you are capable of settling down and thinking in a focused way.

3. **Identify Your Area of Focus:** If you have great focus, but it is concentrated on the wrong things, you will not reach your potential. What are your dreams? What are your talents? What resources do you have at your disposal? What sense of calling do you have on your life? Spend some of your thinking time focused on working through those questions and clarify your goals so that you know where to place your focus.

4. **Focus on Pivotal Decisions:** Our lives are most affected, for good or bad, by just a few key decisions. Focused thinking can help you work through those decisions. Anytime you recognize that an issue or a decision is important, dedicate some focused thinking time for it to give you clarity.

AN EXERCISE IN FOCUSED THINKING

Look at your calendar for the coming week and find a free hour. Mark that as your thinking time. Write it on your calendar, show you're out-of-office or unavailable.

When that time comes, leave behind your phone, your MP3 player, your PDA, your computer, and any other item that can cause distraction. Bring only a pen and a small notebook to jot down your ideas.

Go to your thinking place. If you don't have one, find one. You might find it in your yard, at the local branch of your library, in a public park, in a room in your house, a quiet coffee shop, or even just walking near your office. Use this time to focus your thoughts on one specific problem that needs solving, or a good idea that needs developing.

DISCUSSION QUESTIONS

1. Can you think of an example of a highly focused individual or company that has achieved great success? What was it about their focus that made them successful?
2. Whom do you admire more: people who are highly skilled at one thing or multitalented people who seem capable of tackling nearly anything?
3. How do you think that admiration affects your attitude toward focused thinking?
4. Are you someone who naturally focuses on one thing at a time or someone who tends to jump continually from idea to idea or project to project?
5. Can you give an example of how focused thinking has helped you accomplish a task or solve a problem in the past?
6. What is your greatest obstacle when it comes to focused thinking?
7. What are you willing to do to improve in this area?
8. Are there things others can do to help you become a better focused thinker?

3

Harness Creative Thinking

The joy is in creating, not maintaining.
— VINCE LOMBARDI, NFL HALL OF FAME COACH

Creativity is pure gold, no matter what you do for a living. Annette Moser-Wellman, author of *The Five Faces of Genius,* asserts, *"The most valuable resource you bring to your work and to your firm is your creativity.* More than what you get done, more than the role you play, more than your title, more than your 'output'—it's your ideas that matter."[1] Despite the importance of a person's ability to think with creativity, few people seem to possess the skill in abundance.

If you're not as creative as you would like to be, you can change your way of thinking. Creative thinking isn't necessarily original thinking. In fact, I think people mythologize original thought. Most often, creative thinking is a composite of other thoughts discovered along the way. Even the great artists, whom we consider highly original, learned from their masters, modeled their work on that of others, and brought together a host of ideas and styles to create their own work. Study art, and you will see threads that run through the work of all artists and artistic movements, connecting them to other artists who went before them.

CREATIVE THINKING CASE STUDY

Many people mistakenly believe that if individuals aren't born with creativity, then they will never be creative. But creativity can be cultivated. In fact, some people work so hard to make themselves creative thinkers and spend so much time thinking outside of the box that I'm not sure they even have a box anymore.

I read an article about group of people who do just that. They make up a small marketing company in Richmond, Virginia, called Play. The company is a caldron of creativity: The corner conference room is called the playroom. Employees invent their own titles, and some of the titles they have for themselves are the person "in charge of what's next," the "voice of reason," "check please," and "1.21 jigawatts." They are encouraged to take radical sabbaticals to climb mountains, learn to surf, or do anything else that may spur greater creativity.

When the ideas are flying and everyone's pushing the envelope, employees call that "mojo." When a team hits a wall and deadline is approaching, they "red flag" a project and everyone in the organization pitches in. "No one goes home before the owner of a red-flag project feels comfortable," explains employee Courtney Page, "no matter how long it takes."

The founders of Play have created an incredible environment of creativity. Bill Howland, product manager of the Center for Creative Leadership, which tested Play's ability to foster creativity, said that Play's "scores were off the charts. I have not seen another company with such an open and creative environment in my six years with the center."

The company's values are straightforward: people, play, profit—in that order. Robb Pair, who leads the company's merchandising division, says, "Working at Play really gives me a feeling of 'no limits.' Risk is encouraged, and I have the chance to explore my potential and abilities."

Play cofounder Andy Sefanovich describes how Play has been able to foster such creativity: "What we're doing is building a creative community—not mystifying creativity as a special talent of a chosen few."[2]

And what's their advice to people who want to become more creative, as they are? "Look at more stuff, and think about it harder." That's a formula all of us can learn to embrace.

APPLYING THE CASE STUDY

After reading about Play, answer the following questions:

1. What is your first instinctive reaction to what you read about the company? Did it seem creative or chaotic?

   _____

   _____

   _____

2. What is your opinion about the titles people gave themselves? Did those seem fun or silly?

   _____

   _____

   _____

3. How much of creativity is a willingness to look foolish or silly?

   _____

   _____

   _____

4. How would you respond if your organization or department "red flagged" a project so that everyone was required to pitch in until the project was completed? Would you find that compelling or annoying?

   _____

   _____

   _____

5. What is your general attitude toward creativity and working with creative people? How does that impact your ability to be creative?

   _____

   _____

   _____

HOW CREATIVE THINKING CAN MAKE
YOU MORE SUCCESSFUL

Creativity can improve a person's quality of life. Here are five specific things creative thinking has the potential to do for you:

1. Creative Thinking Adds Value to Everything

Wouldn't you enjoy a limitless reservoir of ideas that you could draw upon at any time? That's what creative thinking gives you. For that reason, no matter what you are currently able to do, creativity can increase your capabilities.

Creativity is being able to see what everybody else has seen and think what nobody else has thought so that you can do what nobody else has done. Sometimes creative thinking lies along the lines of invention, where you break new ground. Other times it moves along the lines of innovation, which helps you to do old things in a new way. But either way, it's seeing the world through sufficiently new eyes so that new solutions appear. That always adds value.

Do you think of yourself as a creative person? How easy or difficult do you find it to tap into your own creativity?

_____

_____

_____

2. Creative Thinking Compounds

Over the years, I've found that

Creative Thinking Is Hard Work

but

Creative Thinking Compounds, Given Enough

Time and Focus

Perhaps more than any other kind of thinking, creative thinking builds on itself and increases the creativity of the thinker. Poet

Maya Angelou observed, "You can't use up creativity. The more you use, the more you have. Sadly, too often creativity is smothered rather than nurtured. There has to be a climate in which new ways of thinking, perceiving, questioning are encouraged." If you cultivate creative thinking in a nurturing environment, there's no telling what kind of ideas you can come up with. (I'll talk more on that later.)

How would you describe your work environment when it comes to creativity?

_____

_____

_____

3. Creative Thinking Draws People to You and Your Ideas

Creativity is intelligence having fun. People admire intelligence, and they are always attracted to fun — so the combination is fantastic. If anyone could be said to have fun with his intelligence, it was Leonardo da Vinci. The diversity of his ideas and expertise staggers the mind. He was a painter, an architect, a sculptor, an anatomist, a musician, an inventor, and an engineer. The term *Renaissance man* was coined because of him.

Just as people were drawn to da Vinci and his ideas during the Renaissance, they are drawn to creative people today. If you cultivate creativity, you will become more attractive to other people, and they will be drawn to you.

Who are the most creative people in your world? What do you admire about their creativity?

_____

_____

_____

4. Creative Thinking Helps You Learn More

Author and creativity expert Ernie Zelinski says, "Creativity is the joy of not knowing it all. The joy of not knowing it all refers to the realization that we seldom if ever have all the answers; we always have the ability to generate more solutions to just about any problem. Being creative is being able to see or imagine a great deal of opportunity to life's problems. Creativity is having options."[3]

It almost seems too obvious to say, but if you are always actively seeking new ideas, you will learn. Creativity is teachability. It's seeing more solutions than problems. And the greater the quantity of thoughts, the greater the chance for learning something new.

Which word do you more readily identify with: expert *or* learner? *How does that help or harm your creativity?*

_____

_____

_____

5. Creative Thinking Challenges the Status Quo

If you desire to improve your world—or even your own situation—then creativity will help you. The status quo and creativity are incompatible. Think about it: if Thomas Edison had valued the status quo over creativity, would he have invented the lightbulb?

Where do you stand in relation to the status quo? In general, do you consider yourself to be satisfied with your life, work, and environment? Or are you someone who is constantly trying to change things? How does this impact your creativity?

_____

_____

_____

WHAT IF YOU BECAME BETTER AT CREATIVE THINKING?

We can only change, grow, and improve in areas where we acknowledge that we need to improve. Think very honestly about yourself when it comes to creative thinking. How much do you need to improve in this area? What might change in your life if you were to start thinking creatively? How would that impact you professionally? Relationally? Financially? Spiritually? Spend some time reflecting and recording your thoughts here.

HOW TO BECOME A CREATIVE THINKER

At this point you may be saying, "Okay, I'm convinced that creative thinking is important. But how do I find the creativity within me? How do I discover the joy of creative thought?" Here are five ways to do it:

1. Remove Creativity Killers

Economics professor and humor author Stephen Leacock said, "Personally, I would sooner have written *Alice in Wonderland* than the whole *Encyclopedia Britannica*." He valued the warmth of creativity over cold facts. If you do, too, then you need to eliminate attitudes that devalue creative thinking.

If you think you have a great idea, don't let yourself or anyone else subject you to creativity killers. After all, you can't do something new and exciting if you force yourself to stay in the same old rut. Don't just work harder at the same old thing. Make a change.

2. Think Creatively by Asking the Right Questions

Creativity is largely a matter of asking the right questions, such as:

- Why must it be done *this* way?
- What is the root problem?
- What are the underlying issues?
- What does this remind me of?
- What is the opposite?
- What metaphor or symbol helps to explain it?
- Why is it important?
- What's the *hardest* or *most expensive* way to do it?
- Who has a different perspective on this?
- What happens if we *don't* do it at all?

Physicist Tom Hirschfield observed, "If you don't ask 'Why this?' often enough, somebody will ask 'Why you?'" If you want to think creatively, you must ask good questions. You must challenge the process.

3. Develop a Creative Environment

Advertising honcho Charlie Brower said, "A new idea is delicate. It can be killed by a sneer or a yawn; it can be stabbed to death by a quip and worried to death by a frown on the right man's brow." Negative environments kill thousands of great ideas every minute.

A creative environment, on the other hand, becomes like a greenhouse where ideas get seeded, sprout up, and flourish. A creative environment:

- **Encourages creativity.** Management expert David Hills says, "Studies of creativity suggest that the biggest single variable of whether or not employees will be creative is whether they perceive they have permission."
- **Places a high value on trust among team members and on individuality.** Creativity always risks failure. That's why trust is so important to creative people.
- **Embraces those who are creative.** Creative people celebrate the offbeat. How should creative people be treated? I take the advice of Tom Peters: "Weed out the dullards, nurture the nuts!"
- **Focuses on innovation, not just invention.** Sam Weston, creator of the popular action figure GI Joe, said, "Truly groundbreaking ideas are rare, but you don't necessarily need one to make a career out of creativity. My definition of creativity is the logical combination of two or more existing elements that result in a new concept."
- **Is willing to let people go outside the lines.** Most limitations we face are not imposed on us by others; we place them on ourselves. Lack of creativity often falls into that category. If you want to be more creative, challenge boundaries.
- **Appreciates the power of a dream.** A creative environment promotes the freedom of a dream. A creative environment allowed Martin Luther King Jr. to speak with passion and declare to millions, "I have a dream," not "I have a goal."

4. Spend Time with Other Creative People

What if the place you work has an environment hostile to creativity and you possess little ability to change it? One possibility is to change jobs. But what if you desire to keep working there despite the negative environment? Your best option is to find a way to spend time with other creative people.

Creativity is contagious. Have you ever noticed what happens during a good brainstorming session? One person throws out an idea. Another person uses it as a springboard to discover another idea. Someone else takes it in yet another, even better direction. Then somebody grabs hold of it and takes it to a whole new level. The interplay of ideas can be electric.

It's a fact that you begin to think like the people you spend a lot of time with. The more time you can spend with creative people engaging in creative activities, the more creative you will become.

5. Get Out of Your Box

Actress Katharine Hepburn remarked, "If you obey all the rules, you miss all the fun." While I don't think it's necessary to break all the rules (many are in place to protect us), I do think it's unwise to allow self-imposed limitations to hinder us. Creative thinkers know that they must repeatedly break out of the box of their own history and personal limitations in order to experience creative breakthroughs.

CREATIVE THINKING ACTION PLAN

1. **Find or Foster a Creative Environment:** Does your work environment naturally encourage creativity or shut it down? If it doesn't encourage creativity, you need to make some changes. First, find other creative people to spend time with. If they can be found in your work environment, great. If not, seek them outside of it.

   Second, do things to improve your current workplace. Use pictures, photos, inspirational objects, toys, or games to promote creative thought. Ask others not to give any negative feedback during brainstorming sessions. Praise and reward creative thinking and innovation. Introduce play if you can. If it's within your power, give people time to go recharge their mental batteries or take them out for experiences together that will stimulate their thinking.

   Some of these ideas may sound frivolous, but creativity leads to innovation, and innovation leads to improved strategies, products, and services within an organization.

2. **Do Something Different:** One of the best ways to stimulate creative thinking is to get out of your routine or out of your area of expertise. Learning opens up your thinking.

   Read books outside of your field. Find a new hobby. Learn a new skill. Do something you've dreamed of doing since you were a child. Vacation in a country with a culture different from your own. Get uncomfortable. Get in over your head. Expose yourself to things that will stretch your mind and get you out of your comfort zone.

3. **Ask Yourself More Questions:** Creativity often comes from asking more questions. You must challenge yourself and others in order to think in different ways.

   Create a list of questions that you can use to stimulate your thinking as you do your everyday work. Use the following list of questions to get you started, but be sure to create your own questions that will help you in your particular field:

Why do I like this idea?
What are the underlying issues involved with it?
What does this remind me of?
What is the opposite?
What metaphor or symbol helps explain it?
What is the value of the idea?
What's the hardest or most expensive way to carry it out?
Who has a different perspective on this?
What happens if I don't do it at all?
In my wildest dreams, what can this idea lead to?

Once you have created the list, put it on an index card or on your phone, iPad, or PDA. You want to be able to carry it with you all the time and refer to it when you are working or in meetings.

AN EXERCISE IN CREATIVE THINKING

1. Think about something that isn't working well for you, something you'd like to change. Give it a title on the line on the following worksheet. Feel free to be clever, or passionate.

2. Inside the box, describe it as it is now, why it isn't working. You could use single words, sentences, draw a pie chart, whatever you feel captures the problem.

3. Now, outside of the box, describe how you would like it to be. Don't worry if it's practical, don't stop to think if it will work. Just put down anything that comes to mind. Use symbols, pictures, abbreviations, create a collage, anything that means something to you.

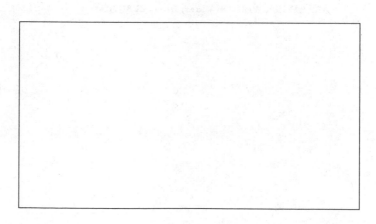

DISCUSSION QUESTIONS

1. When you hear the word *creativity,* what do you think of?
2. On a scale of 1 to 10, how would you rate yourself when it comes to creativity?
3. How important is creativity in your job or profession?
4. Who is the most creative person you know? Describe him or her. What qualities do you admire most?
5. Is there a downside to being a creative person? What negative qualities have you observed in people you think of as being creative?
6. What is your greatest challenge when it comes to creative thinking?
7. When do you feel most creative? How is it impacted by what activities you are engaged in? Is your creativity affected by the time of day? The season of the year? The people you're with?
8. What changes can you make to your environment, working habits, or leisure time that will improve your creative thinking? When will you make those changes?

4

Employ Realistic Thinking

The first responsibility of a leader is to define reality.

— Max De Pree

If you just finished working through the previous chapter on creative thinking, you may be tempted to believe that this chapter on realistic thinking will be contradictory. I say that because early in my career, I avoided realistic thinking because I feared it would stifle my creativity. I've since learned the value of both kinds of thinking.

Reality is the difference between what we wish and what is. You can't ignore that and succeed. It took some time for me to learn that and evolve into a realistic thinker. The process went in phases. First, I did not engage in realistic thinking at all. After a while, I realized that it was necessary, so I began to engage in it occasionally. (But I didn't like it because I thought it was too negative. And anytime I could delegate it, I did.) Eventually, I found that I *had* to engage in realistic thinking if I was going to solve problems and learn from my mistakes. And in time, I became willing to think realistically *before* I got in trouble and make it a continual part of my life. Today, I not only engage in it every day, but I encourage my key leaders to think realistically. We make realistic thinking the foundation of our business because we derive certainty and security from it. I suggest you do the same.

REALISTIC THINKING CASE STUDY

Our country received lessons in realistic thinking following the tragedy of September 11, 2001. The destruction of the World Trade Center buildings in New York City far surpassed any worst-case scenarios that anyone might have envisioned. In the wake of that event, we now find that we don't have the luxury of avoiding or neglecting realistic thinking.

I was reminded of that on Sunday, February 3, 2002, when I attended the first Super Bowl following the September 11 tragedy. The game was in New Orleans, Louisiana. I had been to the big game twice before, rooting for my home team—first San Diego and later Atlanta. And I had seen both teams lose! But I had never been to a game like this.

The occasion had been designated a National Security Special Event. That meant that the U.S. Secret Service would be overseeing it; military personnel would work with local law enforcement; and security would be of the highest caliber. The Secret Service brought in several hundred agents and secured the area. In preparation for the game, access to the Louisiana Superdome was highly restricted, with intensified screening. Officials blocked off roads, closed the nearby interstate, and designated the area a no-fly zone.

We arrived early at the Superdome—officials suggested fans arrive up to five hours ahead of game time—and we immediately saw evidence of the precautionary measures. Eight-foot fences surrounded the whole area, and concrete barriers prevented unauthorized vehicles from getting close to the building. We could see sharpshooters positioned at various locations, including on the roofs of some adjacent buildings. When we reached a gate, police officers and security personnel patted us down and examined everyone's belongings. After that they directed us to go through metal detectors. Only then did they allow us into the stadium.

"That's all well and good," you may be saying, "but what would have happened had there been a terrorist attack?" The Secret Service had that covered, too, because they had prepared for the worst-case scenario. Evacuation plans had been put into place, and personnel at the Superdome had been drilled to make sure everyone knew what to do in case of an emergency.

New Orleans mayor Marc Morial said the day before the Super Bowl, "We want to send a message to all visitors that New Orleans is going to be the safest place in America."[1] We got the message. We didn't feel the least bit worried. That's what happens when leaders recognize the importance of realistic thinking.

APPLYING THE CASE STUDY

As you think about the story of the 2002 Super Bowl, consider these questions:

1. Do the measures that the authorities took to ensure security at the 2002 Super Bowl seem extreme or reasonable in your opinion? Explain.

   _____

   _____

   _____

2. Think about the security measures currently being taken at airports. Do you consider what authorities require to be too strict, realistic, or too loose based on the current threats citizens face today?

   _____

   _____

   _____

3. How would you define realistic thinking? How would you define optimistic thinking? How would you define pessimistic thinking? Do the differences between your three definitions say anything about which direction your thinking leans? Do you tend to be optimistic, pessimistic, or realistic? Explain.

   _____

   _____

   _____

4. What role does realistic thinking play in security issues? In business? In family life? In sports? Is realistic thinking generally a positive trait or a negative one? Explain.

   _____

   _____

   _____

HOW REALISTIC THINKING CAN
MAKE YOU MORE SUCCESSFUL

If you're a naturally optimistic person, as I am, you may not possess a great desire to become a more realistic thinker. But cultivating the ability to be realistic in your thinking will not undermine your faith in people, nor will it lessen your ability to see and seize opportunities. Instead, it will add value to you in other ways:

1. Realistic Thinking Minimizes Downside Risk

Actions always have consequences; realistic thinking helps you to determine what those consequences could be. And that's crucial, because only by recognizing and considering consequences can you plan for them. If you plan for the worst-case scenario, you can minimize the downside risk.

How often do you consider worst-case scenarios in your strategic planning? Does this practice play as prominent a role as your consideration of possible gains? If not, why not?

_____

_____

_____

2. Realistic Thinking Gives You a Target and a Game Plan

I've known businesspeople who were not realistic thinkers. Here's the good news: they were very positive and had a high degree of hope for their business. Here's the bad news: hope is not a strategy.

Realistic thinking leads to excellence in leadership and management because it requires people to face reality. They begin to define their target and develop a game plan to hit it. When people engage in realistic thinking, they also begin to simplify practices and procedures, which results in greater efficiency.

Truthfully, in business only a few decisions are important. Realistic thinkers understand the difference between the important decisions and those that are merely necessary in the normal course of business. The decisions that matter relate directly to your purpose. James Allen was right when he wrote, "Until thought is linked with purpose there is no intelligent accomplishment."[2]

How do you go about recognizing the difference between important decisions and necessary ones?

_____

_____

_____

3. Realistic Thinking Is a Catalyst for Change

People who rely on hope for their success rarely make change a high priority. If you have only hope, you imply that achievement and success are out of your hands. It's a matter of luck or chance. Why bother changing?

Realistic thinking can dispel that kind of wrong attitude. There's nothing like staring reality in the face to make a person recognize the need for change. Change alone doesn't bring growth, but you cannot have growth without change.

Describe how facing reality has helped you to change in the past. Give specific examples.

_____

_____

_____

4. Realistic Thinking Provides Security

Anytime you have thought through the worst that can happen and you have developed contingency plans to meet it, you become more confident and secure. It's reassuring to know that you are unlikely to be surprised. Disappointment is the difference between expectations and reality. Realistic thinking minimizes the difference between the two.

Think of a challenge you are currently facing. Go through the process of thinking through the worst-case scenario. What are all the negative possibilities? Now think of the best-case scenario and all the good it could bring. How prepared do you now feel to face it?

_____

_____

_____

5. Realistic Thinking Gives You Credibility

Realistic thinking helps people to buy in to the leader and his or her vision. Leaders continually surprised by the unexpected soon lose credibility with their followers. On the other hand, leaders who think realistically and plan accordingly position their organizations to win. That gives their people confidence in them.

The best leaders ask realistic questions *before* casting vision. They ask themselves things like:

- Is it possible?
- Does this dream include everyone or just a few?
- Have I identified and articulated the areas that will make this dream difficult to achieve?

If you are a leader and you are currently working on a project or an initiative, ask yourself the three questions listed above and write your detailed answers here. Then consider how your answers will help your leadership.

_____

_____

_____

6. Realistic Thinking Provides a Foundation to Build On

Thomas Edison observed, "The value of a good idea is in using it." The bottom line on realistic thinking is that it helps you to make an idea usable by taking away the wish factor. Most ideas and efforts don't accomplish their intended results because they rely too much on what we wish for rather than what is.

You can't build a house in midair; it needs a solid foundation. Ideas and plans are the same. They need something concrete on which to build. Realistic thinking provides that solid foundation.

Realistic thinking helps you to understand your starting point in any endeavor. Consider a current work goal. What is your starting point? What is your current situation? What difficulties do you think you will face? Take inventory.

---

7. Realistic Thinking Is a Friend to Those in Trouble

If creativity is what you would do if you were unafraid of failure, then reality is dealing with failure when it does happen. Realistic thinking gives you something concrete to fall back on during times of trouble, which can be very reassuring. Certainty in the midst of uncertainty brings stability.

How do you deal with failure? Do you use realistic thinking to look at yourself and examine what went wrong? Give concrete examples. How has your level of willingness to look at hard truths helped or hurt you?

---

8. Realistic Thinking Brings the Dream to Fruition

British novelist John Galsworthy wrote, "Idealism increases in direct proportion to one's distance from the problem." If you don't get close enough to a problem, you can't tackle it. If you don't take a realistic look at your dream — and what it will take to accomplish it — you will never achieve it. Realistic thinking helps to pave the way for bringing any dream to fruition.

Think about a long-term goal or dream you possess that has gone unfulfilled. More than likely you have focused more of your thinking on its benefits than on the reality of what it will take to win it. Spend time looking realistically at what it will take to accomplish it, how long it will take, what resources you possess, what obstacles you face, what steps will be required to reach it, and who might be willing to help.

_____

_____

_____

WHAT IF YOU BECAME BETTER AT
REALISTIC THINKING?

We can only change, grow, and improve in areas where we acknowledge that we need to improve. Think very honestly about yourself when it comes to realistic thinking. How much do you need to improve in this area? What might change in your life if you were to start thinking realistically? How would that impact you professionally? Relationally? Financially? Spiritually? Spend some time reflecting and recording your thoughts here.

HOW TO BECOME A REALISTIC THINKER

Because I'm naturally optimistic rather than realistic, I've had to take concrete steps to improve my thinking in this area. Here are five things I do to improve my realistic thinking. I recommend that you do them, too:

1. Develop an Appreciation for Truth

President Harry S. Truman said, "I never give 'em hell. I just tell the truth and they think it is hell." That's the way many people react to truth. We naturally tend to exaggerate our successes and minimize our failures. And unfortunately, many people today could be described by a quote from Winston Churchill: "Men occasionally stumble over the truth, but most pick themselves up and hurry off as if nothing has happened." If you want to become a realistic thinker, however, you need to get comfortable dealing with the truth and face up to it.

2. Do Your Homework

The process of realistic thinking begins with doing your homework. You must first get the facts. Former governor, congressman, and ambassador Chester Bowles said, "When you approach a problem, strip yourself of preconceived opinions and prejudice, assemble and learn the facts of the situation, make the decision which seems to you to be the most honest, and then stick to it." It doesn't matter how sound your thinking is if it's based on faulty data or assumptions.

3. Think through the Pros and Cons

There's nothing like taking the time to really examine the pros and cons of an issue to give you a strong dose of reality. It rarely comes down to simply choosing the course of action with the greatest number of pros, because all pros and cons do not carry equal weight. But that's not the value of the exercise, anyway. Rather, it helps you to dig into the facts, examine an issue from many angles, and really count the cost of a possible course of action.

4. Picture the Worst-Case Scenario

The essence of realistic thinking is discovering, picturing, and examining the worst-case scenario. Ask yourself questions such as:

- What if sales fall short of projections?
- What if revenue hits rock bottom? (Not an optimist's rock bottom, but real rock bottom!)
- What if we don't win the account?
- What if the client doesn't pay us?
- What if we have to do the job shorthanded?
- What if our best player gets sick?
- What if all the colleges reject my application?
- What if the market goes belly-up?
- What if the volunteers quit?
- What if nobody shows up?

You need to think about worst-case possibilities whether you are running a business, leading a department, pastoring a church, coaching a team, or planning your personal finances. Your goal isn't to be negative or to expect the worst, just to be ready for it in case it happens. That way, you give yourself the best chance for a positive result—no matter what.

5. Align Your Thinking with Your Resources

One of the keys to maximizing realistic thinking is aligning your resources with your objectives. Looking at pros and cons and examining worst-case scenarios will make you aware of any gaps between what you desire and what really is. Once you know what those gaps are, you can use your resources to fill them. After all, that's what resources are for.

REALISTIC THINKING ACTION PLAN

1. **Know Your Wiring:** How difficult is it for you to think in realistic terms? If you are naturally a visionary or a people pleaser or creative (or all three, as I am), you may have a difficult time thinking realistically. Take a look at the following scale and see where you fit on it. Circle the number next to the sentence that best describes you.

   1 I do not engage in realistic thinking.
   2 I do not like realistic thinking.
   3 I will let someone else do realistic thinking.
   4 I will do realistic thinking only after I am in trouble.
   5 I will do realistic thinking before I am in trouble.
   6 I will continually make realistic thinking part of my life.
   7 I will think realistically and encourage my key leaders to do the same.
   8 I will make realistic thinking the foundation of our business.
   9 I derive certainty and security from realistic thinking.
   10 I rely heavily on facts and often make judgments based on the worst-case scenario.

   Your goal should be to move as far as you can down the list. Find two other like-minded people who would also like to grow in the area of realistic thinking, and talk together weekly to challenge one another in this area and hold one another accountable.

2. **Make "Homework" Part of Your Regular Routine:** Most people have to force themselves to think realistically. It doesn't come naturally. If that is true for you, then you need to build it into your regular routine. One way to do that is to plan to research and think through worst-case scenarios every time you take on a project or set goals. Do some homework on what could go wrong, and build that into your planning process.

3. **Rally Your Resources:** For an important current project or goal, after you have thought through all the steps required to complete it, use realistic thinking to consider all the things that could go wrong. Then use both of those lists to allocate your resources. You may find that if you use this process on a regular basis, you will experience fewer delays and monetary shortfalls when you reach the execution phase.

4. **Encourage Truth Tellers:** People need individuals in their lives who are willing to tell them the truth. They need others to be honest with them without being hurtful or vindictive.

   Who in your life fits that description? Are there people around you who are realistic with you? If so, who are they? Talk to them and encourage them to continue being honest with you. If not, start looking for them.

AN EXERCISE IN REALISTIC THINKING

This exercise will require the help of someone you trust completely to be honest with you.

1. Write down your five greatest strengths and five greatest weaknesses.

   _____

   _____

   _____

   _____

   _____

2. Ask a close friend or family member to write down what they consider your five greatest strengths and five greatest weaknesses.

3. Exchange lists. Check those you agree with and put an X by those you disagree with. Ask your friend to do the same.

4. Discuss the lists.

5. Write down how you can better utilize each strength and how you can improve on each weakness.

DISCUSSION QUESTIONS

1. Which kinds of people do you most often enjoy spending time with: optimists, pessimists, or realists? Why?
2. Most people lean toward either optimism or pessimism. Which attitude is more natural for you?
3. Which do you think is the greatest factor when it comes to a person's optimism or pessimism: temperament, experience, or training?
4. What are the benefits of considering the worst-case scenario in any endeavor? What are the negative effects of looking at worst-case scenarios?
5. Is it possible to regularly think through worst-case scenarios and still maintain a generally positive outlook? If not, why not? If so, how?
6. Consider this definition of realistic thinking: neither expecting the worst nor blindly hoping for the best, but instead being cognizant of both and prepared for either. Do you agree with that definition? Explain.
7. Using the definition in the question above, how do you measure up as a realistic thinker?
8. What are you willing and able to do to improve your realistic thinking ability?

Utilize Strategic Thinking

Most people spend more time planning their summer vacation than planning their lives.

— UNKNOWN

When you hear the words *strategic thinking,* what comes to mind? Do visions of business plans dance in your head? Or do you recall some of history's greatest military campaigns: Hannibal crossing the Alps to surprise the Roman army, or the Allies' D-Day invasion of Normandy? Business planning and military action are areas where strategy is certainly important. But the truth is that strategic thinking can make a positive impact on any area of life.

Some people don't plan. Most who do plan their lives one day at a time. Fewer individuals plan their lives one week at a time—they review their calendar for the week, check their appointments, review their goals, and then get to work. Weekly planners generally outachieve most of their daily-planning colleagues. I believe we must try to take planning further. I'll illustrate what I mean by telling you something I do regularly.

At the beginning of every month, I spend half a day working on my calendar to plan for the next forty days. Forty days works for me rather than just thirty, because it helps me get a jump on the next month. I begin by reviewing my travel schedule and planned family activities. Then I review what projects, lessons, and other objectives I want to accomplish. Then I start blocking out days and times for thinking, writing, working, meeting with people, etc. I set times to do fun things, such as seeing a show, watching a ball game, or playing golf. I also set aside small blocks of time to compensate for the unexpected. By the time I'm done, I can tell you nearly everything I'll be doing, almost hour by hour, during the coming weeks. This strategy is one of the reasons I have been able to be highly productive. Strategic thinking has changed my life, and it can change yours, too.

STRATEGIC THINKING CASE STUDY

Evelyn Ryan was a housewife in Defiance, Ohio, in the mid-1950s. She never learned to drive, and she never worked outside of the house after she started having children. In fact, she lived at a time when a mother was expected to stay at home. That might not have been a problem, except that she had ten children, her husband made only a meager living in a machine shop, and he was an alcoholic who drank up about a third of his take-home pay every week.

Anyone who passed Evelyn Ryan on the street in the 1950s likely would not have identified her as an impressive strategic thinker, yet she was. She had to figure out a way to raise her ten children, take care of the house, and bring in enough extra money for the family to survive.

Evelyn lived at a time in America when contests were frequently sponsored by product manufacturers. I was growing up then, so I remember those radio and television announcements inviting people to write in twenty-five words or less why they liked Tide detergent, or asking them to finish a jingle for Dr Pepper.

Evelyn decided to enter as many contests as she could. She had a natural ability with words, and she had cultivated it by working on the local newspaper before she got married. So to her it was a logical plan. Since she couldn't go out to work to earn extra money, she would earn it by entering contests.

But being able to write hundreds of poems, jingles, and promotional paragraphs while managing, feeding, and doing laundry for a family of twelve required great strategy. Evelyn had elaborate systems for finding and storing contest entry blanks and proofs of purchase. Then she had to write while she worked. For this, she carried a notebook around everywhere, doing her most productive writing while ironing.

Evelyn's strategic thinking wasn't restricted to the logistics of being able to write. She was also very strategic about *what* she wrote. The words she wrote for any given contest were chosen very carefully. Her daughter Terry recalled how Evelyn approached the task:

> Contesting, as she always said, required more than collecting box tops and being clever. There was *form* to consider (some

contests required the use of specific words, or gave points for the use of product-related words in an entry), *product focus* (was it aimed at families, at young men, at children?), and *judges*. The advertising agency hired...to judge the contest was always a more important consideration for entrants than the sponsor or the product. Each agency had its preference for rhyme or prose, for humorous or straight material.[1]

Evelyn learned the likes and dislikes of every ad agency that administered contests, and her strategy served her well. Over the years she won washers and dryers, dozens of other large and small appliances, two brand-new cars (which they sold), many small cash awards, and some large cash awards. The first big cash prize she used as a down payment for a house so that the family of twelve could move out of a two-bedroom rental.

When failure isn't an option, nothing serves a person better than strategic thinking. Evelyn Ryan would have been content to write an occasional poem and submit it to her local paper. But she needed to do something to help her family survive. "A husband and father like my dad was never going to change," her daughter observed. "The only hope for our family depended on the way *she* could change and raise happy and healthy kids to boot."[2] And Evelyn succeeded. Not only did she keep her family afloat; she helped it to become successful. Seven of her children graduated from college, one earning a PhD and another a law degree.

APPLYING THE CASE STUDY

Evelyn Ryan's story is an inspiration. Reflect on the way she used strategic thinking to her advantage:

1. Evelyn Ryan could have easily thought of herself as a victim. She could have left her husband. She could have given up or turned to drugs or alcohol. But instead, she tenaciously used strategic thinking to improve her life. What do you think separates people who act as she did from others who choose a less positive path?

   _____

   _____

   _____

2. How might things have turned out for Evelyn Ryan had she been less strategic in her thinking when approaching the contests?

   _____

   _____

   _____

3. Can you think of any modern-day equivalents to the contests Evelyn Ryan was taking advantage of? If so, are there people pursuing them? Do these modern-day equivalents also require strategic thinking?

   _____

   _____

   _____

4. Do you have a similar level of urgency to what Evelyn Ryan experienced in any area of your life? If so, are you using strategic thinking to help you solve it? If not, how do you create the energy and tenacity that she had to help you accomplish your goals and dreams?

   _____

   _____

   _____

HOW STRATEGIC THINKING CAN
MAKE YOU MORE SUCCESSFUL

Strategic thinking helps a person to plan, become more efficient, maximize strengths, and find the most direct path toward achieving any objective. The benefits of strategic thinking are numerous. Here are a few of the reasons you should adopt it as one of your thinking tools:

1. Strategic Thinking Simplifies the Difficult

Strategic thinking is really nothing more than planning on steroids. Spanish novelist Miguel de Cervantes said, "The man who is prepared has his battle half fought." Strategic thinking takes complex issues and long-term objectives, which can be very difficult to address, and breaks them down into manageable sizes. Anything becomes simpler when it has a plan!

Strategic thinking can also help you simplify the management of everyday life. I do that by using systems, which are little more than good strategies repeated. I am well-known among pastors and other speakers for my filing system. Writing a lesson or speech can be difficult. But I use my system to file quotes, stories, and articles, so when I need something to flesh out or illustrate a point I simply go to one of my twelve hundred files, and in minutes I find a good piece of material that works. Just about any difficult task can be made simpler with strategic thinking.

What systems have you discovered or developed to help you become organized and efficient in your life? In what areas are you lacking systems that might help you?

_____

_____

_____

2. Strategic Thinking Prompts You to Ask the Right Questions

Do you want to break down complex or difficult issues? Then ask questions. Strategic thinking forces you through this process.

Take a look at the following questions developed by my friend Bobb Biehl, the author of *Masterplanning*:

- **Direction:** What should we do next? Why?
- **Organization:** Who is responsible for what? Who is responsible for whom? Do we have the right people in the right places?
- **Cash:** What is our projected income, expense, net? Can we afford it? How can we afford it?
- **Tracking:** Are we on target?
- **Overall Evaluation:** Are we achieving the quality we expect and demand of ourselves?
- **Refinement:** How can we be more effective and more efficient (move toward the ideal)?[3]

These may not be the only questions you need to ask to begin formulating a strategic plan, but they are certainly a good start.

Use Bobb Biehl's questions as a template to create your own set of strategic questions related to the vision of your department, organization, or career direction.

_____

_____

_____

3. Strategic Thinking Prompts Customization

General George S. Patton observed, "Successful generals make plans to fit circumstances, but do not try to create circumstances to fit plans."

All good strategic thinkers are precise in their thinking. They try to match the strategy to the problem, because strategy isn't a one-size-fits-all proposition. Sloppy or generalized thinking is an enemy of achievement. The intention to customize in strategic thinking forces a person to go beyond vague ideas and engage in specific ways to go after a task or problem. It sharpens the mind.

What problem or challenge are you currently facing that is being addressed by general rules, policies, or procedures that

would be better addressed by customized strategic thinking?
Plan to spend some time working on it, and do the work needed
to be able to implement your plan.

_____

_____

_____

4. Strategic Thinking Prepares You Today for an Uncertain Tomorrow

Strategic thinking is the bridge that links where you are to where you want to be. It gives direction and credibility today and increases your potential for success tomorrow. It is, as Mary Webb suggested, like saddling your dreams before you ride them.

Think about your greatest dreams and aspirations. Do you have
a strategic plan for achieving them? If not, why not? How might
strategic thinking help you?

_____

_____

_____

5. Strategic Thinking Reduces the Margin of Error

Any time you shoot from the hip or go into a totally reactive mode, you increase your margin for error. It's like a golfer stepping up to a golf ball and hitting it before lining up the shot. Misaligning a shot by just a few degrees can send the ball a hundred yards off target. Strategic thinking, however, greatly reduces that margin for error. It lines up your actions with your objectives, just as lining up a shot in golf helps you to put the ball closer to the pin. The better aligned you are with your target, the better the odds that you will be going in the right direction.

How consistently do you utilize strategic thinking to help you
achieve your objectives in your professional life? Your personal
life? Your financial goals? Your recreational activities?

_____

_____

_____

_____

6. Strategic Thinking Gives You Influence with Others

One executive confided in another: "Our company has a short-range plan and a long-range plan. Our short-range plan is to stay afloat long enough to make it to our long-range plan." That's hardly a strategy, yet that's the position where some business leaders put themselves. There's more than one problem with neglecting strategic thinking in that way. Not only does it fail to build the business, but it also loses the respect of everyone involved with the business.

The one with the plan is the one with the power. It doesn't matter in what kind of activity you're involved. Employees want to follow the business leader with a good business plan. Volunteers want to join the pastor with a good ministry plan. Children want to be with the adult who has the well-thought-out vacation plan. If you practice strategic thinking, others will listen to you and they will want to follow you. If you possess a position of leadership in an organization, strategic thinking is essential.

Do the key people in your life—colleagues, bosses, employees, family, and friends—consider you to be strategic and well organized? Or would they more likely label you as impulsive and flaky? Why? How has this impacted your personal and professional relationships?

_____

_____

_____

WHAT IF YOU BECAME BETTER
AT STRATEGIC THINKING?

We can only change, grow, and improve in areas where we acknowledge that we need to improve. Think very honestly about yourself when it comes to strategic thinking. How much do you need to improve in this area? What might change in your life if you were to start thinking strategically? How would that impact you professionally? Relationally? Financially? Spiritually? Spend some time reflecting and recording your thoughts here.

HOW TO BECOME A STRATEGIC THINKER

To become a better strategic thinker, able to formulate and implement plans that will achieve the desired objective, take the following guidelines to heart:

1. Break Down the Issue

The first step in strategic thinking is to break down an issue into smaller, more manageable parts so that you can focus on each part more effectively. How you break down an issue is up to you, whether it's by function, timetable, responsibility, purpose, or some other method. The point is that you need to break it down. Only one person in a million can juggle it all in his head and think strategically to create solid, viable plans.

2. Ask Why Before How

When most people begin using strategic thinking to solve a problem or plan a way to meet an objective, they often make the mistake of jumping the gun and trying immediately to figure out *how* to accomplish it. Instead of asking *how,* they should first ask *why.* If you jump right into problem-solving mode, how are you going to know all the issues?

Steel magnate Eugene G. Grace said, "Thousands of engineers can design bridges, calculate strains and stresses, and draw up specifications for machines, but the great engineer is the man who can tell whether the bridge or the machine should be built at all, where it should be built, and when."

Besides addressing the reasons for decisions, asking *why* helps you to open your mind to possibilities and opportunities. The size of an opportunity often determines the level of resources and effort that you must invest. Big opportunities allow for big decisions. If you jump to *how* too quickly, you might miss that.

3. Identify the Real Issues and Objectives

William Feather, author of *The Business of Life,* said, "Before it can be solved, a problem must be clearly defined." Too many people rush to solutions, and as a result they end up solving the wrong problem. To avoid that, ask probing questions to expose the real issues. Begin by asking, "What else could be the real issue?" You should also remove any personal agenda. More than almost anything else, that can cloud your judgment. Discovering your real situation and objectives is a major part of the battle. Once the real issues are identified, the solutions are often simple.

4. Review Your Resources

I already mentioned how important it is to be aware of your resources, but it bears repeating. A strategy that doesn't take resources into account is doomed to failure. Take an inventory. How much time do you have? How much money? What kinds of materials, supplies, or stock do you have? What are your other assets? What liabilities or obligations will come into play? Which people on the team can make an impact? You know your own organization and profession. Figure out what resources you have at your disposal.

5. Develop Your Plan

How you approach the planning process depends greatly on your profession and the size of the challenge that you're planning to tackle, so it's difficult to recommend many specifics. However, no matter how you go about planning, take this advice: start with the obvious. When you tackle an issue or plan that way, it brings unity and consensus to the team, because everyone sees those things. Obvious elements build mental momentum and initiate creativity and intensity. The best way to create a road to the complex is to build on the fundamentals.

6. Put the Right People in the Right Place

It's critical to include your team as part of your strategic thinking. Even the best strategic thinking won't help if you don't take into account the people part of the equation. Look at what happens if you miscalculate:

- **Wrong Person:** Problems instead of Potential
- **Wrong Place:** Frustration instead of Fulfillment
- **Wrong Plan:** Grief instead of Growth

Everything comes together, however, when you put together all three elements: the right person, the right place, and the right plan.

7. Keep Repeating the Process

My friend Olan Hendrix remarked, "Strategic thinking is like showering—you have to keep doing it." Little things—such as filing, cleaning, planning a calendar, shopping, etc.—can be accomplished easily through systems and personal discipline. But major issues need major strategic thinking time. What the legendary football coach Fielding Yost said is really true: "The will to win is not worth a nickel unless you have the will to prepare." If you want to be an effective strategic thinker, then you need to become a continuous strategic thinker.

STRATEGIC THINKING ACTION PLAN

1. **Strategize Yourself First:** Are you currently doing things that are not strategically smart for you to be doing? You may be spending more hours than you should working in areas of weakness, just as I did on my first job. Take some time to create an inventory of your personal strengths, then match it against your calendar and to-do list or a log tracking your activities over a month. If your talents and resources don't match up with your activities, then you need to dedicate some strategic-thinking time to figuring out how you can make a transition—even if it means changing jobs, organizations, or careers.

2. **Always Ask** *Why:* Might you be missing opportunities because you are too quick to ask *how* instead of *why*? Think about major objectives that you are currently planning for. Set aside one hour a day for the next week to ask nothing but *why* questions concerning your objective. You can invite people to brainstorm with you at some point, but spend the majority of the time just thinking alone. Be particularly alert for any opportunities that might be present that you had not yet seen.

   Once you've got the hang of this practice, put strategic-thinking time on your calendar on a weekly basis. You'll be amazed by the impact one or two hours of thinking can make on productivity.

3. **Balance Intuition and Strategy:** Most people tend to lean toward either intuition or strategy. Both are important. Most of the time, you want to go with your strength. However, even the most intuitive person should not neglect strategy.

   Even when you are fairly certain that your gut is right, if a process or issue is large and complex, break it down into smaller parts. Even if this doesn't help you, it will help many of the people you lead.

4. **Find a Strategic Mentor:** Try to find someone whose ability to strategize is stronger than your own. If you have a track

record of misdiagnosing problems and applying the wrong kinds of solutions to them, then you are in great need of a mentor who is a good strategic thinker. Find someone whose wisdom and discernment you admire and who has a history of successful problem solving. Ask your mentor to sit in as an observer on problem-solving meetings. Take problems to him or her to get ideas. Learn how this person thinks so that you can begin developing similar thinking strategies.

AN EXERCISE IN STRATEGIC THINKING

1. In one sentence on the lines below, state your goal.
2. List the first five action items you can think of that you will need to achieve your goal.
3. For each of the five action items, list the first three steps you need to take.

MY GOAL:

_____

_____

ACTION ITEMS

A. _____
    1. _____
    2. _____
    3. _____
B. _____
    1. _____
    2. _____
    3. _____
C. _____
    1. _____
    2. _____
    3. _____
D. _____
    1. _____
    2. _____
    3. _____
E. _____
    1. _____
    2. _____
    3. _____

DISCUSSION QUESTIONS

1. How would you define strategic thinking?
2. What role does strategic thinking play in your profession or field?
3. Some people make a distinction between strategy, which is an overall plan created beforehand, and tactics, which are actions taken in the moment to adjust to what's happening while the plan is being implemented. Which are you better at?
4. What role does strategic thinking play when it comes to working with people? Is it manipulation to apply strategy to people? If not, why not? If so, when does it become manipulation?
5. Would you rather develop strategies or work with people? Why?
6. How high would you rate your ability as a strategic thinker? Upon what do you base your rating? In what area is your strategic thinking at its best?
7. What's the best way for you to improve your ability to think strategically?
8. What's the value in partnering people who are strong at strategy with those who aren't? Do you see the potential for creating those kinds of partnerships in your area? Which people would you put together so that both they and the organization benefit?

6

Explore Possibility Thinking

Nothing is so embarrassing as watching someone do something that you said could not be done.

— SAM EWING

In 1970, when I was twenty-three years old, I read a book that made a major impact on how I dream. It was called *Move Ahead with Possibility Thinking* by Robert Schuller. As a young pastor in my first church, I was thrilled to read about how Schuller overcame seemingly impossible circumstances to build a huge church in Garden Grove, California. When I read the following words, my world changed: "The greatest churches have yet to be organized."

Even as a child, I was a positive person. After all, I had grown up in the household of a father who had taught himself to be a positive thinker. But Schuller's book still had a huge impact on my life. The day I read those words, what had been my wildest dreams looked tame. If you embrace possibility thinking, your dreams will go from molehill to mountain size, and because you believe in possibilities, you put yourself in position to achieve them.

POSSIBILITY THINKING CASE STUDY

In 1975 filmmaker George Lucas went to see Doug Trumbull, the special-effects expert who had worked on *2001: A Space Odyssey,* the first film that gave space travel a realistic feel and look. Lucas had a vision for a new film he wanted to make. It was to be a story in a science-fiction setting that would be swashbuckling adventure, Arthurian quest, and Western-style showdown—all rolled into one. Lucas spoke to Trumbull because he wanted to create scenes with fast-moving ships zooming through space, similar to the way airplanes are filmed in a dogfight. It was something that had never been done. Up to that point, space movies looked like either the original, technically unsophisticated *Star Trek* television series or the slow-moving but realistic *2001.*

Author and filmmaker Thomas G. Smith, who has led special-effects units in Hollywood, says, "The experienced visual effects people didn't take George seriously. They told him such rapid movement would cause a strobing effect on the screen."[1] In other words, they told the young Lucas that it was technically impossible, and it couldn't be done. Then they sent Lucas on his way.

Lucas was not about to give up. In his mind's eye, he could see what he wanted, and he believed it could be done. He hired John Dykstra, a young filmmaker who had worked with Trumbull, and created his own special-effects company in order to create the images he wanted. He called it Industrial Light and Magic (ILM).

Dykstra, who had some experience using computers while filming, worked with a team of technicians to design and build a studio. Then they began working to make the impossible possible. Through good thinking and trial and error, they worked for almost two years to create what Lucas wanted. The result was the movie *Star Wars.* At the time, it was the most technically innovative movie ever made.

When the movie made money—lots of money—Lucas realized that he would be able to complete the other *Star Wars* movies he had envisioned. And ILM, the company he had founded specifically to produce *Star Wars*'s special effects, would help him create these other movies. But in the process, ILM also grew into something more. It became the company that made other filmmakers' visions come to life—it made their possibilities possible.

Industrial Light and Magic has set the standard for special effects for over three decades. It has gone on to provide special effects for eight of the ten highest-grossing movies of all time, and in the process it has won twelve Academy Awards. But first and foremost, it is George Lucas's tool to help him realize his vision. The technology keeps advancing, and the effects keep getting more sophisticated, yet the company's capabilities never surpass the possibilities Lucas sees in his mind.

In the late 1990s, as Lucas began working on the second trilogy of *Star Wars* movies, he again wanted to do the impossible. "When we started *Episode I: The Phantom Menace*, we said, 'Okay, now we're gonna do it the way we always wanted to do it. We've got the money, we've got the knowledge—this is it.'"[2] The trick, Lucas said, was "learning the difference between the impossible and the merely never-before-done-or-imagined."[3] For Lucas, most things are merely never-before-done-or-imagined, because to him anything is possible. That's how it is for a proponent of possibility thinking.

APPLYING THE CASE STUDY

Many creative people seem to possess the ability to harness possibility thinking. As you think about George Lucas and *Star Wars*, answer these questions:

1. Did the movie *Star Wars* have any effect on you personally? If so, explain.

   _____

   _____

   _____

2. Many of the movies people watch today utilize special effects that were developed as a result of *Star Wars*. Were you aware of the innovative nature of that movie and its impact on the film industry? How did possibility thinking affect that? How might the industry be different today had it not been for George Lucas?

   _____

   _____

   _____

3. For whom do you believe possibility thinking was more difficult? The visionary filmmaker or the technical expert who had to create the technology? Why?

   _____

   _____

   _____

4. Is there a correlation between the size of the vision and the extent of the innovation needed to execute it? What other factors come into play?

   _____

   _____

   _____

HOW POSSIBILITY THINKING CAN
MAKE YOU MORE SUCCESSFUL

People who embrace possibility thinking are capable of accomplishing tasks that seem impossible because they believe in solutions. Here are several benefits you will receive from becoming a possibility thinker:

1. Possibility Thinking Increases Your Possibilities

When you believe you can do something difficult—and you succeed—many doors open for you. When George Lucas succeeded in making *Star Wars,* despite those who said the special effects he envisioned couldn't be done, many other possibilities opened up to him. Industrial Light and Magic, the company he created to produce those "impossible" special effects, became a source of revenue to help underwrite his other projects. He was able to produce merchandising tie-ins to his movies, thus bringing in another revenue stream to fund his moviemaking. But his confidence in doing the difficult has also made a huge impact on other moviemakers and a whole new generation of moviegoers.

Popular culture writer Chris Salewicz asserts, "At first directly through his own work and then via the unparalleled influence of ILM [Industrial Light and Magic], George Lucas has dictated for two decades the essential broad notion of what is cinema."[4] If you open yourself up to possibility thinking, you open yourself up to many other possibilities.

> *How likely are you to take no for an answer when it comes to your dreams? Do you get easily discouraged when people tell you something can't be done? Or does the opposition fire you up? Explain.*

_____

_____

_____

2. Possibility Thinking Draws Opportunities and People to You

The case of George Lucas helps you to see how being a possibility thinker can create new opportunities and attract people. People who think big attract big people to them. If you want to achieve big things, you need to become a possibility thinker.

What kinds of people are drawn to you? Are they positive or negative? What does your answer say about your present attitude?

_____

_____

_____

3. Possibility Thinking Increases Others' Possibilities

Big thinkers who make things happen also create possibilities for others. That happens, in part, because it's contagious. You can't help but become more confident and think bigger when you're around possibility thinkers.

Which people in your life have helped to create opportunities for you because they had a positive attitude in general or because they believed in you in particular? What kind of impact has that made?

_____

_____

_____

4. Possibility Thinking Allows You to Dream Big Dreams

No matter what your profession, possibility thinking can help you to broaden your horizons and dream bigger dreams. Professor David J. Schwartz believes, "Big thinkers are specialists in creating positive, forward-looking, optimistic pictures in their own minds and in the minds of others." If you embrace possibility thinking, your dreams will go from molehill to mountain size, and because you believe in possibilities, you put yourself in a position to achieve them.

Open yourself up to greater possibilities. What dream might you embrace and pursue if there were no chance that you could fail?

_____

_____

5. Possibility Thinking Makes It Possible to Rise Above Average

During the 1970s, when oil prices went through the roof, automobile makers were ordered to make their cars more fuel efficient. One manufacturer asked a group of senior engineers to drastically reduce the weight of cars they were designing. They worked on the problem and searched for solutions, but they finally concluded that making lighter cars couldn't be done, would be too expensive, and would present too many safety concerns.

What was the automaker's solution? Giving the problem to a group of less experienced engineers. The new group found ways to reduce the weight of the company's automobiles by hundreds of pounds. Because they thought that solving the problem was possible, it was. Every time you remove the label of *impossible* from a task, you raise your potential from average to off the charts.

In what area of your life are you in greatest need of possibility thinking? Where do you feel you have few options or opportunities? Where would you most like to see your future open up?

_____

_____

_____

6. Possibility Thinking Gives You Energy

A direct correlation exists between possibility thinking and the level of a person's energy. Who gets energized by the prospect of losing? If you know something can't succeed, how much time and energy are you willing to give it? Nobody goes looking for a lost cause. You invest yourself in what you believe can succeed. When you embrace possibility thinking, you believe in what you're doing, and that gives you energy.

In what area of your life do you find yourself needing energy the most? Have you considered that a lack of hope could be the source of your low energy level? Explain.

_____

_____

_____

7. Possibility Thinking Keeps You from Giving Up

Above all, possibility thinkers believe they can succeed. Denis Waitley, author of *The Psychology of Winning*, says, "The winners in life think constantly in terms of 'I can, I will and I am.' Losers, on the other hand, concentrate their waking thoughts on what they should have done, or what they don't do." If you believe you can't do something, then it doesn't matter how hard you try, because you've already lost. If you believe you can do something, you have already won much of the battle.

In general, what percentage of your time and energy is focused on the past and regret? What percentage is focused on the present? What percentage on future possibilities? Fill in the pie chart below.

_____% *past*

_____% *present*

_____% *future*

Now think about how much of your present focus connects to future possibilities (versus simply getting done things that must *be done for the purpose of maintenance). If there is not a strong correlation between present tasks and future possibilities, you probably need to increase your possibility thinking dramatically.*

WHAT IF YOU BECAME BETTER
AT POSSIBILITY THINKING?

We can only change and grow in areas where we acknowledge that we need to improve. Think very honestly about yourself when it comes to possibility thinking. How much do you need to improve in this area? What might change in your life if you were to start thinking more positively? How would that impact you professionally? Relationally? Financially? Spiritually? Spend some time reflecting and recording your thoughts here.

HOW TO BECOME A POSSIBILITY THINKER

If you are a naturally positive person who already embraces possibility thinking, then you're already tracking with me. However, if your thinking runs toward pessimism, let me ask you a question: how many highly successful people do you know who are continually negative? How many *impossibility* thinkers are you acquainted with who achieve big things? None!

People with an it-can't-be-done mind-set have two choices. They can expect the worst and continually experience it; or they can change their thinking. That's what George Lucas did. Believe it or not, even though he is a possibility thinker, he is not a naturally positive person. He says, "I am very cynical, and as a result, I think the defense I have against it is to be optimistic."[5] In other words, he chooses to think positively.

If you want possibility thinking to work for you, then begin by following these suggestions:

1. Stop Focusing on the Impossibilities

The first step in becoming a possibility thinker is to stop yourself from searching for and dwelling on what's wrong with any given situation. Sports psychologist Bob Rotella recounts, "I tell people: If you don't want to get into positive thinking, that's okay. Just eliminate all the negative thoughts from your mind, and whatever's left will be fine."

If possibility thinking is new to you, you're going to have to give yourself a lot of coaching to eliminate some of the negative self-talk you may hear in your head. When you automatically start listing all the things that can go wrong or all the reasons something can't be done, stop yourself and say, "Don't go there." Then ask, "What's right about this?" That will help to get you started. And if negativity is a really big problem for you and pessimistic things come out of your mouth before you've even thought them through, you may need to enlist the aid of a friend or family member to alert you every time you utter negative ideas.

2. Stay Away from the "Experts"

Critics, who often like to call themselves experts, do more to shoot down people's dreams than just about anybody else. In contrast, possibility thinkers are very reluctant to dismiss anything as impossible. Rocket pioneer Wernher von Braun said, "I have learned to use the word *impossible* with the greatest caution." If you feel you must take the advice of an expert, then strengthen your resolve by remembering the words of John Andrew Holmes, who asserted, "Never tell a young person that something cannot be done. God may have been waiting centuries for somebody ignorant enough of the impossible to do that thing." If you want to achieve something, give yourself permission to believe it is possible—no matter what experts might say.

3. Look for Possibilities in Every Situation

Becoming a possibility thinker is more than just refusing to let yourself be negative. It's looking for positive possibilities despite the circumstances. I recently heard Don Soderquist, former president of Wal-Mart, tell a wonderful story that illustrates how a person can find positive possibilities in any situation. Soderquist had gone with Sam Walton to Huntsville, Alabama, to open several new stores. While there, Walton suggested they visit the competition. At the first store they visited, Soderquist was appalled by the clutter, the dirt, and the scarcity of both customers and staff.

He told Walton as much when they met on the sidewalk outside later. But Walton immediately asked, "Don, did you see the pantyhose rack?" Soderquist was puzzled, but Walton continued, "When we get back, I want you to call that manufacturer and have him...put that rack in our stores. It's absolutely the best I've ever seen."

Then Walton pointed out the cosmetics displays—specifically cosmetics for people with darker skin. "Did you see the ethnic cosmetics?" he asked. "In our stores we have four feet of ethnic cosmetics. These people had twelve feet of it....I wrote down the distributor of some of those products. When we get back, I want you to get a hold of our cosmetic buyer and get these people in. We absolutely need to expand our ethnic cosmetics."

Walton saw the same store that day, but he focused on different things. Soderquist explains, "It's so easy to go and look at what other people do badly. But one of the leadership characteristics of vision that he showed me, and I'll never forget it, is look for the good in what other people are doing and apply it."[6]

It doesn't take a genius IQ or twenty years of experience to find the possibility in every situation. All it takes is the right attitude, and anybody can cultivate that.

4. Dream One Size Bigger

One of the best ways to cultivate a possibility mind-set is to prompt yourself to dream one size bigger than you normally do. Let's face it: most people dream too small. They sell themselves short. Henry Curtis advises, "Make your plans as fantastic as you like, because twenty-five years from now, they will seem mediocre. Make your plans ten times as great as you first planned, and twenty-five years from now you will wonder why you did not make them fifty times as great."

If you push yourself to dream more expansively, to imagine your organization one size bigger, to make your goals at least a step beyond what makes you comfortable, you will be forced to grow. And it will set you up to believe in greater possibilities.

5. Question the Status Quo

Most people want their lives to keep improving, yet they value peace and stability at the same time. But you can't improve and remain unchanged at the same. Growth means change. Change requires challenging the status quo. If you want greater possibilities, you can't settle for what you have now.

As you explore greater possibilities for yourself, your organization, or your family—and please be aware that others will challenge you for it—take comfort in knowing that *right now,* as you read this, other possibility thinkers across the country and around the world are thinking about curing cancer, developing new energy sources, feeding hungry people, and improving quality of life. They are challenging the status quo against the odds—and you should, too.

6. Find Inspiration from Great Achievers

You can learn a lot about possibility thinking by studying great achievers. I mentioned George Lucas. Perhaps he doesn't appeal to you, or you don't like the movie industry. (Personally, I'm not a big science fiction fan, but I admire Lucas as a thinker, creative visionary, and businessperson. And his movies are fun.) Find some achievers you admire and study them. Look for people with the attitude of Robert F. Kennedy, who was paraphrasing George Bernard Shaw when he said, "Some men see things as they are and say, 'Why?' I dream of things that never were and say, 'Why not?'"

POSSIBILITY THINKING ACTION PLAN

1. **Change Your Focus:** Where does your thinking usually go? Do you focus on the possibilities? Do you dream about the positive things that could result from your efforts? Or do you naturally think about all the things that could go wrong?

   Some people who are naturally good at realistic thinking have a tough time with possibility thinking. If that's you, then you need to change your focus. You can still think about worst-case scenarios, but you need to do two additional things regularly. First, give as much thinking time to best-case scenarios as you do worst-case scenarios. That should help to keep you from being too negative. Second, employ positive thinking to come up with solutions for the things that you've discovered by thinking of the worst-case scenarios. Do this enough and you can steer yourself toward being more positive.

2. **Dream Big:** If you have a natural bent toward dreaming big dreams, fantastic. Keep dreaming and be sure to write down those dreams. If you aren't used to dreaming big, start now. Give yourself dreaming time. Let your mind go. If you need to, go back to your childhood and think about what you dreamed about back then. What were the things you really wanted to do? Recapture those ideas, explore them, and dream about them again. The idea is to start dreaming again.

   The dreams you had earlier in life may not be possible for you now. (Although many are, if you're willing and able to pay the price.) So, focus primarily on what you really want to do now. What is your dream? If you didn't fear failure or being laughed at, what would you do today? Write it out and start thinking about what it would take to go after it.

3. **Avoid Negative People:** The world is full of dream killers and habitually negative people. If you want to become a possibility thinker, then you need to try to avoid them if possible. If it's not possible, then minimize your contact with them. And you should definitely avoid sharing your dreams with them.

The one exception to this rule is if the negative person is a close family member. If your spouse or one of your children is very negative, then you need to work together to try to reduce their negativity. This will be very difficult, but it is something worth fighting for.

4. **Read Stories of Inspiringly Positive People:** This week, read a biography of someone you admire. If you have the time and energy, read two or three about the same person. Make notes concerning how that person harnessed the energy of possibility thinking in his or her life. Then find three to five principles or practices from that person's life that you can apply to your own.

_____

_____

_____

_____

_____

_____

_____

_____

_____

_____

_____

_____

_____

_____

_____

_____

_____

AN EXERCISE IN POSSIBILITY THINKING

1. Write down a problem you've been struggling with, something that seems impossible to solve.

_____

_____

_____

2. Complete the sentences that follow.

But what if . . .

_____

_____

_____

What if . . .

_____

_____

_____

What if . . .

_____

_____

_____

What if . . .

_____

_____

_____

And what if . . .

_____

_____

_____

DISCUSSION QUESTIONS

1. Do you see any difference between possibility thinking and positive thinking? Explain.
2. What is your attitude toward possibility thinkers? Do you see them as naïve speakers of positive platitudes or as people more likely to succeed at their goals?
3. Who is the most positive person you admire? Tell about him or her.
4. Does possibility thinking actually increase your chances of success? Or do you think it's just a game people play with themselves to keep from feeling down or depressed?
5. Do you see any correlation between possibility thinking and a person's ability to see solutions to problems?
6. Have you made attempts to balance possibility thinking and realistic thinking? If so, what were they? How successful were they?
7. When others talk about positive possibilities, are you more likely to support them or criticize them (either openly or in your head)? Why do you think you react the way you do?
8. Are you willing to look for, share, and promote possibilities, even in the face of others' cynicism or criticism? If not, how do you think this will affect your life and career?

7

Learn from Reflective Thinking

To doubt everything or to believe everything are two equally convenient solutions; both dispense with the necessity of reflection.
— JULES-HENRI POINCARÉ

The pace of our society does not encourage reflective thinking. Most people would rather act than think. Now, don't get me wrong. I'm a person of action. I have very high energy and I like to see things accomplished. But I'm also a reflective thinker. Through reflective thinking, my goal is to learn from my successes and mistakes, discover what I should try to repeat, and determine what I should change. Reflective thinking is always a valuable exercise. By mentally visiting past situations, you can think with greater understanding.

Ultimately, reflective thinking has three main values: it gives perspective within context; it allows continual connection with life's journey; and it provides counsel and direction concerning the future. I've found it to be an invaluable tool for my personal growth, and I believe it can be the same for you. Few things in life can help a person to learn and improve the way reflective thinking can.

REFLECTIVE THINKING CASE STUDY

As I work on this chapter, I am sitting at my desk in my home office, and I am surrounded with items that help me to reflect on an almost continual basis and to get my work done quickly and efficiently.

On the left side of my desk, I have folders for the project that I am currently working on. Each folder is a different color so that I can quickly identify it. Green holds ideas, quotes, and stories for current teaching and writing. Purple is for personal issues and ideas related to my companies. A blue folder contains thoughts I'm gathering for my next book. Each folder has a list of questions handwritten on the outside to prompt my thinking or keep me on track as I collect ideas.

On the far side of my desk, across from me, are pictures of people who are important to me. There's a picture of my wife, Margaret, taken on a trip to Europe years ago, a picture of my beautiful daughter, Elizabeth, taken when she was a senior in high school, and another of Joel Porter, my son, standing with me next to a monument of John Wesley in England. There are up to date pictures of both of our children with their spouses, Elizabeth with Steve and Joel Porter with Elisabeth (yes, it's confusing that our daughter and daughter-in-law have the same name). And of course, there are numerous pictures of my grandchildren, the apples of their grandfather's eye! As I look at them, I am constantly reminded of what's most important in my life.

On the right side of my desk are file folders containing the main lectures I will be giving this year. I like to keep them close so that I can continually update them and refer to them. The ones for events that I will be leading in the next two weeks are in yellow folders so that I can focus additional attention on them.

And right in front of me are three items within easy reach. The first is the legal pad I'm writing on now. Whatever project I'm currently working on stays front and center—even if I go to an appointment in the morning or quit for the day. I want to be able to dive into the material in a moment. Next to that is my communication pad. If there's an experience I want to share with Margaret, or if I need to remember to tell something to my assistant, Linda, I jot it down there. The third item is a small leather-bound pad that I call my idea pad. I try to capture what I call my thought of the day (I try to produce one good thought each day) or any other ideas I want to be able to reflect on.

I like to think of my desk as being like a stove. It's always got a lot of things cooking on it. Each item has its place, and at any given moment, I might take a "pot" from a back burner, where it has been simmering for days, weeks, or even months, and move it to the front burner so that I can actively work on it or even finish it off.

Reflective thinking is a major part of my life and has been for decades. I'm constantly reflecting and reviewing my life so that I can keep growing and celebrating victories. I got into the habit of thinking reflectively when I was a pastor. Because churches function on a weekly cycle, I used to spend time every Sunday night reviewing the previous week, reflecting on the effectiveness of the weekend's activities, and evaluating everything in order to prepare for the coming week. As I experienced the value of that kind of reflection, I began to spend at least a few minutes every day reflecting. Each time I ask myself three questions:

- What did I learn today?
- What should I share?
- What must I do?

I've found that asking myself these questions helps me to stay disciplined and accountable for how I spend my time.

Once every year, at the end of December, I spend time reflecting on the past year. First, I gather together my calendar for the year and review how I spent my time. I think and process and pray about the year. Then I capture some thoughts on paper.

As I go through this process, my goal is to reflect on how I spent a year of my life, learn from my successes and mistakes, discover what I should try to repeat, and determine what I should change in the coming year. It is always a valuable process. By visiting past situations in your mind, you can think with greater understanding. Reflective thinking is like the Crock-Pot of the mind. It encourages your thoughts to simmer until they're done.

APPLYING THE CASE STUDY

As you consider the case study based on my method of reflective thinking, answer the following questions:

1. The author took a very personal approach to reflective thinking in this chapter. Why do you think he did that?

    _____

    _____

    _____

2. Why do you think the author has so many photographs in the area where he does his reflective thinking? If you have a specific place where you do your thinking, what kinds of items do you have there? Why have you chosen them?

    _____

    _____

    _____

3. What kind of a role does reflective thinking take in the author's profession of writing and speaking? What kind of a role should it play in your profession? If it's not normally considered important for the work you do, is there a way you could incorporate it to your advantage?

    _____

    _____

    _____

4. The author mentioned reflecting every day at the end of the day, every week when he was a pastor, and at the end of every year. What natural rhythms of your life invite reflective thinking? What can you do to make yourself more likely to make the most of them?

    _____

    _____

    _____

HOW REFLECTIVE THINKING CAN
MAKE YOU MORE SUCCESSFUL

Most people don't spend a great deal of time in reflective thinking. Why? Because it doesn't sound very exciting. Reviewing your mistakes and your problems in a systematic way isn't appealing to most people. But it can have a great return in your life. Here's why:

1. Reflective Thinking Gives You True Perspective

When our children were young and still lived at home, we used to take them on wonderful vacations every year. When we got home, they always knew that I was going to ask them two questions: "What did you like best?" and "What did you learn?" It didn't matter whether we went to Walt Disney World or Washington, D.C.

I always asked those questions. Why? Because I wanted them to reflect on their experiences. Children don't naturally grasp the value (or cost) of an experience unless prompted. They take things for granted. I wanted my children to appreciate our trips and to learn from them. When you reflect, you are able to put an experience into perspective. You are able to evaluate its timing. And you are able to gain a new appreciation for things that before went unnoticed. Most people are able to recognize the sacrifices of their parents or other people only when they become parents themselves. That's the kind of perspective that comes with reflection.

In what area of your life do you need better perspective? Who or what are you taking for granted? Give those areas some reflective thinking time.

_____

_____

_____

2. Reflective Thinking Gives Emotional Integrity to Your Thought Life

Few people have good perspective in the heat of an emotional moment. Most individuals who enjoy the thrill of an experience try to go back and recapture it without first trying to evaluate it. (It's one of the reasons our culture produces so many thrill seekers.)

Likewise, those who survive a traumatic experience usually avoid similar situations at all costs, which sometimes ties them into emotional knots.

Reflective thinking enables you to distance yourself from the intense emotions of particularly good or bad experiences and see them with fresh eyes. You can see the thrills of the past in the light of emotional maturity and examine tragedies in the light of truth and logic. That process can help a person to stop carrying around a bunch of negative emotional baggage.

President George Washington observed, "We ought not to look back, unless it is to derive useful lessons from past errors, and for the purpose of profiting by dear bought experience." Any feeling that can stand up to the light of truth and can be sustained over time has emotional integrity and is therefore worthy of your mind and heart.

Is there a positive emotional experience that you have been trying to recapture? Is your desire to recapture it healthy? Reflect on the experience and the actions you've taken since to recapture that feeling. Evaluate it. Determine whether you need to change what you are doing.

_____

_____

_____

Is there a negative emotional experience that has caused you to avoid people or certain situations? Is your avoidance wise or unhealthy? Reflect on that and determine how to proceed in the future.

_____

_____

_____

3. Reflective Thinking Increases Your Confidence in Decision Making

Have you ever made a snap judgment and later wondered if you did the right thing? Everybody has. Reflective thinking can help to diffuse that doubt. It also gives you confidence for the next decision.

Once you've reflected on an issue, you don't have to repeat every step of the thinking process when you're faced with it again. You've got mental road markers from having been there before. That compresses and speeds up thinking time—and it gives you confidence. And over time, it can also strengthen your intuition.

Take some time to reflect and evaluate a major decision you have recently made. Was it a good decision? Did you use a process to make the decision? Is that process something you can and should use again? Are there similar situations that are likely to come up in the future that will allow you to use that process again to save you time and energy?

---

4. Reflective Thinking Clarifies the Big Picture

When you engage in reflective thinking, you can put ideas and experiences into a more accurate context. Reflective thinking encourages us to go back and spend time pondering what we have done and what we have seen. If a person who loses his job reflects on what happened, he may see a pattern of events that led to his dismissal. He will better understand what happened, why it happened, and what things were his responsibility. If he also looks at the incidents that occurred afterward, he may realize that in the larger scheme of things, he's better off in his new position because it better fits his skills and desires. Without reflection, it can be very difficult to see that big picture.

Set aside some time to review the previous week, previous month, and previous year of your life. Use your calendar to help jog your memory. If you have been keeping to-do lists or writing out goals, use them as well. Evaluate your efforts based not only on a job description or set of goals, but on your hopes, dreams, calling, and purpose. Based on those, how are you doing?

_____

_____

_____

5. Reflective Thinking Takes a Good Experience and Makes it a Valuable Experience

When you were just starting out in your career, did it seem that few people were willing to give someone without experience an opportunity? At the same time, could you see people who had been in their jobs twenty years yet who did their work poorly? If so, that probably frustrated you.

Playwright William Shakespeare wrote, "Experience is a jewel, and it had need be so, for it is often purchased at an infinite rate." Yet experience alone does not add value to a life. It's not necessarily experience that is valuable; it's the insight people gain because of their experience. Reflective thinking turns experience into insight.

Mark Twain said, "We should be careful to get out of an experience only the wisdom that is in it—and stop there; lest we be like the cat that sits down on a hot stove-lid. She will never sit down on a hot stove-lid again—and that is well; but also she will never sit down on a cold one any more."[1] An experience becomes valuable when it informs or equips us to meet new experiences. Reflective thinking helps to do that.

Identify one of the best experiences you've had in the past year. How much time have you spent analyzing it? Not just fondly remembering what happened, but evaluating it? Set aside some time to pick it apart and figure it. Then determine what you need to do, in light of what you learned, to have similar positive experiences in the future.

_____

_____

_____

WHAT IF YOU BECAME BETTER AT REFLECTIVE THINKING?

We can only change, grow, and improve in areas where we acknowledge that we need to improve. Think very honestly about yourself when it comes to reflective thinking. How much do you need to improve in this area? What might change in your life if you were to start thinking reflectively? How would that impact you professionally? Relationally? Financially? Spiritually? Spend some time reflecting and recording your thoughts here.

HOW TO BECOME A REFLECTIVE THINKER

If you are like most people in our culture today, you probably do very little reflective thinking. If that's the case, it may be holding you back more than you think. Take to heart the following suggestions to increase your ability to think reflectively:

1. Set Aside Time for Reflection

Greek philosopher Socrates observed, "The unexamined life is not worth living." For most people, however, reflection and self-examination don't come naturally. It can be a fairly uncomfortable activity for a variety of reasons: they have a hard time staying focused; they find the process dull; or they don't like spending a lot of time thinking about emotionally difficult issues. That's why if you are going to be able to do any reflective thinking, you have to carve out time for it.

2. Remove Yourself from Distractions

As much as any other kind of thinking, reflection requires solitude. Distraction and reflection simply don't mix. It's not the kind of thing you can do well near a television, in a cubicle, while the phone is ringing, or with children in the same room.

To do this, I've regularly separated myself from distractions for short blocks of time: an hour outside on a rock in my backyard; a few hours in a comfortable chair in my office; or while swimming laps. The place doesn't matter—as long as you remove yourself from distractions and interruptions.

3. Regularly Review Your Calendar or Journal

Most people use their calendar as a planning tool, which it is. But few people use it as a reflective thinking tool. What could be better, however, for helping you to review where you have been and what you have done—except maybe a journal?

Calendars and journals remind you of how you've spent your time, show you whether your activities match your priorities, and help you see whether you are making progress. They also offer you an opportunity to recall activities that you might not have had the time to reflect on previously. Some of the most valuable thoughts you've ever had may have been lost because you didn't give yourself the reflection time you needed.

4. Ask the Right Questions

The value you receive from reflecting will depend on the kinds of questions you ask yourself. The better the questions, the more gold you will mine from your thinking. When I reflect, I think in terms of my values, relationships, and experiences. Here are some sample questions:

- **Personal Growth:** What have I learned today that will help me grow? How can I apply it to my life? When should I apply it?
- **Adding Value:** To whom did I add value today? How do I know I added value to that person? Can I follow up and compound the positive benefit he or she received?
- **Leadership:** Did I lead by example today? Did I lift my people and organization to a higher level? What did I do and how did I do it?
- **Personal Faith:** Did I represent God well today? Did I practice the Golden Rule? Have I "walked the second mile" with someone?
- **Marriage and Family:** Did I communicate love to my family today? How did I show that love? Did they feel it? Did they return it?
- **Inner Circle:** Have I spent enough time with my key players? What can I do to help them be more successful? In what areas can I mentor them?
- **Discoveries:** What did I encounter today to which I need to give more thinking time? Are there lessons to be learned? Are there things to be done?

How you organize your reflection time is up to you. You may want to adapt my pattern to your own values. Or you can try another system that works better for you. The main thing is to create questions that work for you, and write down any significant thoughts that come to you during the reflection time.

5. Cement Your Learning through Action

Writing down the good thoughts that come out of your reflective thinking has value, but nothing helps you to grow like putting those thoughts into action. To do that, you must be intentional. When you read a good book, for example, there are always good thoughts, quotes, or lessons that you can take away from it and use yourself. I always mark the takeaways in a book and then reread them when I'm done with the book. When I listen to a message, I record the takeaways so that I can file them for future use. When I go to a seminar, I take good notes, and I use a system of symbols to cue me to do certain things:

- An arrow like this → means to look at this material again.
- An asterisk like this * next to a marked section means to file it according to the subject noted.
- A bracket like this [means that I want to use what's marked in a lecture or book.
- An arrow like this ↑ means this idea will take off if I work at it.

When most people go to a conference or seminar, they enjoy the experience, listen to the speakers, and sometimes even take notes. But nothing happens after they go home. They like many of the concepts they hear, but when they close their notebooks, they don't think about them again. When that happens, they receive little more than a temporary surge of motivation. When you go to a conference, revisit what you heard, reflect on it, and then put it into action—it can change your life.

REFLECTIVE THINKING ACTION PLAN

1. **Reflect Daily:** Create a daily reflection time to help you learn from the events of your day and to capture your ideas. Set aside a regular time and place to do your reflecting. Practice the discipline of reflective thinking daily for twenty-one days.

2. **Ask Yourself the Right Questions:** One of the most important things you can do is figure out what questions to ask yourself during your reflective thinking times. Review the questions given as examples in the chapter. Then create your own set of questions. Begin by creating general questions to be used after any event or meeting. Then create more specific questions related to your values and relationships.

3. **Review Your Calendar:** At the end of this month, set aside a block of two to four hours to do a review of your calendar from the past thirty days. Review your appointments. Check your to-do lists. Figure out where you spent your time and whether you did so wisely. As you look at individual entries, ask yourself:

   - What went right?
   - What went wrong?
   - What did I learn?
   - What can I do differently next time?

   Don't forget to write down insights to be filed and action points to be completed.

4. **Learn from Great Thinkers:** In what area of your life do you need more input from great thinkers? Your profession? Your spiritual life? Relationships? Identify an area. Then get recommendations from family, friends, and colleagues on books, articles, webcasts, blogs, audio lessons, DVDs, etc., that will expand your thinking. Create a timetable for learning new ideas, thinking reflectively to apply them to your life, and creating action items to implement them.

AN EXERCISE IN REFLECTIVE THINKING

Examine your calendar/schedule for the past seven days. Be sure to note both what you had planned and what you actually achieved. Then ask yourself:

What did I do that matched my priorities?

_____

_____

_____

What on this list helped me achieve progress toward my goals? How?

_____

_____

_____

What do I need to spend more time thinking about in order to learn?

_____

_____

_____

DISCUSSION QUESTIONS

1. What factors in current society and culture work against reflective thinking?
2. Who is the best reflective thinker you know? What have you learned from him or her?
3. Does your current work environment encourage or discourage reflective thinking?
4. How much time do you normally spend in reflective thinking? What does it look like? Where do you do it? Do you schedule it or does it just naturally happen?
5. What helps you to be more effective when you think reflectively?
6. In what area of your life are you most likely to engage in reflective thinking? In what area are you least likely? Why?
7. If reflective thinking is something you have not practiced much in the past, do you think that has held you back? If so, how? If you have spent a good amount of time in reflective thinking, how has it helped you?
8. What steps are you willing to take in order to become better at reflective thinking? Be specific.

8

Question Popular Thinking

I'm not an answering machine, I'm a questioning machine. If we have all the answers, how come we're in such a mess?
— Douglas Cardinal

Economist John Maynard Keynes, whose ideas profoundly influenced economic theory and practices in the twentieth century, asserted, "The difficulty lies, not in the new ideas, but in escaping from the old ones." Going against popular thinking can be difficult, whether you're a businessperson bucking company tradition, a pastor introducing new types of music to his church, a new mother rejecting old wives' tales handed down from her parents, or a teenager ignoring currently popular styles.

Many of the ideas in this book go against popular thinking. If you value popularity over good thinking, then you will severely limit your potential to learn the types of thinking encouraged by this book.

Popular thinking is...

- Too average to understand the value of Good Thinking.
- Too inflexible to realize the impact of Changed Thinking.
- Too lazy to master the process of Intentional Thinking.
- Too small to see the wisdom of Big-Picture Thinking.
- Too satisfied to unleash the potential of Focused Thinking.
- Too traditional to discover the joy of Creative Thinking.
- Too naïve to recognize the importance of Realistic Thinking.
- Too undisciplined to release the power of Strategic Thinking.

- Too limiting to feel the energy of Possibility Thinking.
- Too trendy to embrace the lessons of Reflective Thinking.
- Too shallow to question the value of Popular Thinking.
- Too proud to encourage the participation of Shared Thinking.
- Too self-absorbed to experience the satisfaction of Unselfish Thinking.
- Too uncommitted to enjoy the return of Bottom-Line Thinking.

If you want to become a good thinker, then start preparing yourself for the possibility of becoming unpopular.

QUESTIONING POPULAR THINKING CASE STUDY

Up until December 18, 1998, I took my health almost for granted. I was fifty-one years old, my energy level was still very high, and I had never experienced any kind of medical problem. But on the night of my company's Christmas party, I suffered a serious heart attack. My life has changed a lot since then. Now I watch my diet, I exercise every day, and I am even more intentional in expressing my love to the important people in my life. That experience has also made me much more aware of issues related to health. That was how I came to read about Paul Ridker, a cardiologist who went against popular thinking and who is changing the way doctors think about patients' risk of heart attacks.

Ridker became interested in medicine because as a child he suffered from a rare disorder. Doctors were eventually able to cure him, but in the meantime the experience immersed him in the world of medicine at a tender age, and it became his passion.

After receiving his undergraduate degree from Brown University, he went to Harvard Medical School for a medical degree and then a master of public health degree. Today he is an associate professor of medicine at Harvard Medical School and the director of the Center for Cardiovascular Disease Prevention at Brigham and Women's Hospital in Boston.

Popular thinking among physicians has been that the best predictor of heart attacks was high cholesterol in a patient's blood. But about half of all heart attacks occur in people with normal cholesterol levels. With this in mind, Ridker wondered if another cause could be found.

Ridker's early research had indicated that inflammation of the arteries might be responsible, so he began a large-scale study to gather data for his theory. At this point he confronted another popular belief: that the kind of low levels of inflammation he desired to track couldn't be detected. "There were many naysayers," says Ridker.[1] Yet he persevered until he found a way to measure inflammation.

What he found was that a substance called C-reactive protein is always present in the blood of people with a high risk of suffering a heart attack. Tracking that substance is as reliable and inexpensive as checking cholesterol. And in fact, it is a better predictor of heart problems than elevated LDL (bad) cholesterol.

For many years, heart disease has been the number one killer of men and women in the United States. And before Ridker's discovery, half the people who were strong candidates to die of heart attacks had no good way to find out they were susceptible. Ridker has helped to change that. Because he was willing to question popular thinking and go in another direction, fewer people are likely to die of heart disease in coming years.

APPLYING THE CASE STUDY

As you reflect on the story of Dr. Ridker, answer the following questions:

1. Paul Ridker is obviously an intelligent person to have become a cardiologist and to have made such medical breakthroughs regarding heart attacks. Do you think his ability to question popular thinking was a matter of intellect, education, observation, attitude, or some other quality? Explain.

_____

_____

_____

2. Ridker's ideas went against the accepted thinking of the entire medical profession. How does a person distinguish between sound commonsense thinking and unfounded popular thinking?

_____

_____

_____

3. What role does intuition play in questioning popular thinking? What role does common sense play?

_____

_____

_____

4. What accepted practice in your profession do you suspect needs to be questioned? How can you go about researching alternatives? If you were successful in finding alternate approaches to your issue, what kind of resistance would you expect to face from your colleagues?

_____

_____

_____

HOW QUESTIONING POPULAR THINKING
CAN MAKE YOU MORE SUCCESSFUL

There are many good reasons for questioning popular thinking and many benefits that come from it. Here are a few:

1. Popular Thinking Sometimes Means Not Thinking

My friend Kevin Myers sums up the idea of popular thinking by saying, "The problem with popular thinking is that it doesn't require you to think at all." If you accept common wisdom without question, it means you didn't think about it.

Good thinking is hard work. If it were easy, everybody would be a good thinker. Unfortunately, many people try to live life the easy way. They don't want to do the hard work of thinking or pay the price of success. It's easier to do what other people do and hope that *they* thought it out.

Look at the stock market recommendations of some experts. By the time they publish their picks, the opportunity has already passed. The people who are going to make money on the stocks they recommend have already done so by the time the general public hears about it. When people blindly follow a trend, they're not doing their own thinking.

In what areas of your life do you take too many things for granted without investigating them yourself? What should you start to do differently to address it?

_____

_____

_____

2. Popular Thinking Offers False Hope

Benno Müller-Hill, a professor in the University of Cologne genetics department, tells how one morning in high school he stood last in a line of forty students in the school yard. His physics teacher had set up a telescope so that his students could view a planet and its moons. The first student stepped up to the telescope. He looked through it, but when the teacher asked if he could see anything, the boy said no; his nearsightedness hampered his view. The teacher showed him how to adjust the focus, and the boy finally said he could see the planet and moons. One by one, the students stepped up to the telescope and saw what they were supposed to see. Finally, the second to last student looked into the telescope and announced that he could not see anything.

"You idiot," shouted the teacher, "you have to adjust the lenses."

The student tried, but he finally said, "I still can't see anything. It is all black."

The teacher, disgusted, looked through the telescope himself, and then looked up with a strange expression. The lens cap still covered the telescope. None of the students had been able to see anything![2]

Many people look for safety and security in popular thinking. They figure that if a lot of people are doing something, then it must be right. It must be a good idea. If most people accept it, then it probably represents fairness, equality, compassion, and sensitivity, right? Not necessarily.

Popular thinking said the earth was the center of the universe, yet Copernicus studied the stars and planets and proved mathematically that the earth and the other planets in our solar system revolved around the sun. Popular thinking said surgery didn't require clean instruments, yet Joseph Lister studied the high death rates in hospitals and introduced antiseptic practices that immediately saved lives. Popular thinking said that women shouldn't have the right to vote, yet people like Emmeline Pankhurst and Susan B. Anthony fought for and won that right. Popular thinking put the Nazis into power in Germany, yet Hitler's regime murdered millions and nearly destroyed Europe. We must always remember there is a huge difference between acceptance and intelligence. People may say that there's safety in numbers, but that's not always true. Sometimes it's painfully obvious that popular thinking isn't good and right. Other times it's less evident.

What current thinking in our society is offering false hope to people? Explain. What is likely to happen as a result? What actions are you taking to keep yourself from following this pop-

ular trend? Are there things you could or should be doing to help others avoid it?

_____

_____

_____

3. Popular Thinking Is Slow to Embrace Change

Popular thinking loves the status quo. It puts its confidence in the idea of the moment, and holds on to it with all its might. As a result, it resists change and dampens innovation. Donald M. Nelson, former president of the Society of Independent Motion Picture Producers, criticized popular thinking when he asserted, "We must discard the idea that past routine, past ways of doing things, are probably the best ways. On the contrary, we must assume that there is probably a better way to do almost everything. We must stop assuming that a thing which has never been done before probably cannot be done at all."

Have you become too complacent in any area of your professional life? If so, what negative impact is it having on your effectiveness? What can you do to challenge the status quo and become more innovative?

_____

_____

_____

4. Popular Thinking Brings Only Average Results

The bottom line? Popular thinking brings mediocre results. Here is popular thinking in a nutshell:

Popular = Normal = Average

It's the least of the best and the best of the least. We limit our success when we adopt popular thinking. It represents putting in the least energy to just get by. You must reject common thinking if you want to accomplish uncommon results.

How dedicated are you to achieving uncommon results? How willing are you to leave your comfort zone—physically, mentally, emotionally, and spiritually—in order to be your best? What do you need to do to jolt yourself out of complacency?

_____

_____

_____

WHAT IF YOU BECAME BETTER AT
QUESTIONING POPULAR THINKING?

We can only change, grow, and improve in areas where we acknowledge that we need to improve. Think very honestly about yourself when it comes to questioning popular thinking. How much do you need to improve in this area? What might change in your life if you were to start asking more questions about popular thinking? How would that impact you professionally? Relationally? Financially? Spiritually? Spend some time reflecting and recording your thoughts here.

HOW TO BECOME A QUESTIONING THINKER

Popular thinking has often proved to be wrong and limiting. Questioning it isn't necessarily hard, once you cultivate the habit of doing so. The difficulty is in getting started. Begin by doing the following things:

1. Think Before You Follow

Many individuals follow others almost automatically. Sometimes they do so because they desire to take the path of least resistance. Other times they fear rejection. Or they believe there's wisdom in doing what everyone else does. But if you want to succeed, you need to think about what's best, not what's popular.

Challenging popular thinking requires a willingness to be unpopular and go outside of the norm. Following the tragedy of September 11, 2001, for example, few people willingly chose to travel by plane. But that was the best time to travel: crowds were down, security was up, and airlines were cutting prices. About a month after the tragedy, my wife, Margaret, and I heard that Broadway shows had lots of open seats and many New York hotel rooms remained empty. Popular thinking said, *Stay away from New York.* Instead, we used that as an opportunity. We got cheap plane tickets to the city, booked a room in a great hotel for about half price, and got tickets to the most sought-after shows, including *The Producers.* As we took our seats in the theater, we sat next to a woman beside herself with excitement.

"I can't believe I'm finally here," she said to us. "I've waited so long. This is the best show on Broadway—and the hardest to get tickets to." Then she turned to look me in the eye and said, "I've had my tickets for a year and a half, waiting to see this show. How long ago did you get yours?"

"You won't like my answer," I replied.

"Oh, come on," she said. "How long?"

"I got mine five days ago," I answered.

She looked at us in horror. We got to see the show only because we were willing to go against popular thinking.

As you begin to think against the grain of popular thinking, remind yourself that...

- Unpopular thinking, even when resulting in success, is largely underrated, unrecognized, and misunderstood.
- Unpopular thinking contains the seeds of vision and opportunity.
- Unpopular thinking is required for all progress.

The next time you feel ready to conform to popular thinking on an issue, stop and think. You may not want to create change for its own sake, but you certainly don't want to blindly follow just because you haven't thought about what's best.

2. Appreciate Thinking That Is Different from Your Own

One of the ways to embrace innovation and change is to learn to appreciate how others think. To do that, you must continually expose yourself to people different from yourself. Spend time with people who have different backgrounds, education levels, professional experiences, personal interests, etc. You will think like the people with whom you spend the most time. If you spend time with people who think out of the box, you're more likely to challenge popular thinking and break new ground.

3. Continually Question Your Own Thinking

Let's face it, anytime we find a way of thinking that works, one of our greatest temptations is to go back to it repeatedly, even if it is no longer as effective. The greatest enemy to tomorrow's success is sometimes today's success. My friend Andy Stanley once taught a leadership lesson called "Challenging the Process." He described how progress must be preceded by change, and he pointed out many of the dynamics involved in questioning popular thinking. In an organization, he said, we should remember that every tradition was originally a good idea—and perhaps even revolutionary. But every tradition may not be a good idea for the future.

In your organization, if you were involved in putting into place what currently exists, then it's likely that you will resist change— even change for the better. That's why it's important to challenge your own thinking. If you're too attached to your own thinking and how everything is done now, then nothing will change for the better.

4. Try New Things in New Ways

When was the last time you did something for the first time? Do you avoid taking risks or trying new things? One of the best ways to get out of the rut of your own thinking is to innovate. You can do that in little, everyday ways: Drive to work a different way from normal. Order an unfamiliar dish at your favorite restaurant. Ask a different colleague to help you with a familiar project. Take yourself off of autopilot.

Unpopular thinking asks questions and seeks options. Most people are more satisfied with old problems than committed to finding new solutions.

How you go about doing new things in new ways is not as important as making sure you do it. (Besides, if you try to do new things in the same way that everyone else does, are you really going against popular thinking?) Get out there and do something different today.

5. Get Used to Being Uncomfortable

When it comes right down to it, popular thinking is comfortable. It's like an old recliner adjusted to all the owner's idiosyncrasies. The problem with most old recliners is that their owners haven't *looked* at them lately. If they did, they'd agree that it's time to get a new one! If you want to reject popular thinking in order to embrace achievement, you'll have to get used to being uncomfortable.

If you embrace unpopular thinking and make decisions based upon what works best and what is right rather than what is commonly accepted, know this: in your early years you won't be as wrong as people think you are. In your later years, you won't be as right as people think you are. And all through the years, you will be better than you thought you could be.

QUESTION POPULAR THINKING ACTION PLAN

1. **Get Uncomfortable:** Make being uncomfortable normal to you. How? Do something every day in a way different from what you're used to. Drive to the office or grocery store a different way every day this week. Arrange your day in an order different from how you usually do. Go on a different kind of date with your partner. Go to a concert featuring music different from what you generally like. Take up a hobby that humbles you. Change your attitude toward new things. Do that and it will not only help you to question popular thinking, but it will also keep you from getting old, not matter your age.

2. **Learn from Others Outside of Your Expertise:** Appreciate how other people think by getting into the head of an innovative thinker. Browse biographies and pick one written about someone outside of your field. If you're someone who loves numbers and facts, read about an artist. If you're artistic, read a business biography. If you avoid politics, read about a politician. You get the idea. Take your mind where it doesn't ordinarily go, and try to appreciate how the subject of the biography thought. Shake up your mind!

3. **Shake Things Up at Work:** In response to the case study, I asked you to think about accepted practices in your profession that needed to be changed. Now try doing something about them. Come up with ten alternatives to a work practice that currently isn't yielding the results you want. Enlist others to help you think through which has the greatest potential to solve the problem. Then create a plan to help you implement the new practice or procedure. Measure its value based entirely on results, and be willing to try something else if it fails.

4. **Make Changes at Home:** We all have things in our lives that are overdue for change. Take time to challenge popular thinking at home to bring the same kind of innovation and improvement that you desire at work. Enlist family members to help you come up with ideas and implement them.

AN EXERCISE IN QUESTIONING POPULAR THINKING

Write down a belief, prejudice, or tradition from your youth that you gladly no longer embrace. (It could be anything from a racist attitude to the tradition of opening gifts on Christmas Eve.)

_____

_____

_____

This was probably the popular way of thinking in your family. What person, event, or information prompted you to consider a change?

_____

_____

_____

In what ways was the transition uncomfortable?

_____

_____

_____

How did you overcome resistance and doubt (from others or even from within)?

_____

_____

_____

In what ways have you benefited from questioning popular thinking in this area?

_____

_____

_____

DISCUSSION QUESTIONS

1. What are some of the trends that are popular today? Which have you followed? Which leave you cold? Which do you think are destructive?

2. Of the trends you discussed, which have been long lasting? Which do you think will continue for a long time?

3. Is susceptibility to trends and popular thinking dependent on a person's age? In other words, are people more susceptible during certain phases of their life? Explain.

4. What kind of people do you find are most likely to question popular thinking? What kind are most likely to follow it?

5. In what areas of your life are you most likely to question popular thinking? In what areas are you most likely to go with the flow?

6. Can you think of a time when you questioned popular thinking with excellent results? Describe that time. What were the results? What caused you to think in a different way?

7. What kinds of pressure do you currently face that may be preventing you from going against established thinking and practices?

8. What do you stand to lose by accepting popular thinking? What do you have to gain by opposing it? Are you willing to pay the price to buck the status quo? Explain.

Benefit from Shared Thinking

None of us is as smart as all of us.

— KEN BLANCHARD

No matter what you're trying to accomplish, you can do it better with shared thinking. That belief is one of the reasons I spend much of my life teaching leadership. Good leadership helps to pull together the right people at the right time for the right purpose so that everybody wins. I'm such a strong believer in shared thinking that I even engage in that process when writing a book.

Most people think a book is the brainchild of a single mind. Sometimes that's true, especially among fiction writers and poets (although Stephen King, possibly the most popular novelist of our time, attributes much of his success to his relationship with his wife). And every book is aided by the work of an editor. Like anything else, I believe a book is better when it is the product of shared thinking.

When I began working on this book, I spent a lot of time in reflective thinking to consider the thinking habits of successful people (in addition to my own). Then I developed an outline. But it wasn't long before I engaged other good thinkers in the process. Early on, I kicked ideas around with my writer, Charlie Wetzel, and my publisher, Rolf Zettersten. It was during these early stages that we identified the title of the book.

Once we landed on the title and basic outline for the book, I assembled a team of about a dozen good creative thinkers to brainstorm more ideas for the book. Some of these people I consulted individually, but I brought the majority of them into a room for a wonderful time of synergistic thinking. Then my research assistant started pulling together story ideas and information. And as Charlie and I got each chapter done, we got valuable feedback from our wives, helping us discover things we missed. And I also enlisted a few individuals with expertise to give feedback on specific chapters.

Could I have written this book all by myself? Certainly. Is it better because I asked people to help me by contributing their ideas? Definitely! My friends and colleagues make me better than I am alone.

You can receive the same kinds of benefits in your field. All it takes is the right people and a willingness from you and them to participate in shared thinking.

SHARED THINKING CASE STUDY

In early 2002, I was invited to meet and spend time with one of the greatest basketball coaches of all time: Pat Summitt of the University of Tennessee Lady Vols. I'm a lover of basketball, so of course I was excited to meet Coach Summitt. Who wouldn't be? She's received more honors than any other coach except John Wooden! Here is a sampling of what she has achieved:

- Winner of 8 NCAA Titles (1987, 1989, 1991, 1996, 1997, 1998, 2007, 2008)
- Winner of 15 SEC Championships
- Coached a perfect season in 1997–98 (39-0)
- Inducted into the Basketball Hall of Fame (2000)
- Inducted into the Women's Basketball Hall of Fame (1999)
- Named Naismith Women's Collegiate Coach of the Century (Wooden was the Men's Honoree)
- Winner of the John Bunn Award (1990)
- Her Lady Vols named ESPN Team of the Decade (1990s)
- Past Lady Vols Players include 12 Olympians, 19 Kodak All-Americans, 74 All-SEC Players, and 25 professionals
- Coached Women's U.S. Olympic Team to first Gold Medal (1984)
- Youngest coach to reach 300 victories (at age 37)
- One of 17 college coaches to have won 700 or more games
- Too many "Coach of the Year" honors to list

When I went up to Knoxville, Tennessee, I knew I was in for a great experience. I got to spend time with Pat in her office talking about leadership and teamwork. Then she had me speak to the Lady Vols team as "guest coach" before their game with Old Dominion. During the game, I sat right behind the bench. And at halftime, I got to join her and the team in the locker room.

A number of things struck me about Pat. First, she's very warm but extremely intense and competitive. A quote from her book, *Reach for the Summit,* tells you everything you need to know about her desire to win. She says, "I have never had a losing season, at anything. In every basketball season I have participated in, I ended up with a winning record."[1]

Second, she's a leader through and through. You can see it in how she runs the team and interacts with her assistant coaches. She's very strategic in her communication with each player, watching and listening to make sure they're tracking with her. Too many coaches, she says, try to give instruction to their players when there's no established foundation of understanding.

But I'll tell you the thing that struck me the most about her. As strong as her personality and leadership ability are, she chooses to practice shared thinking. Here's how she structures halftime in the locker room: In the beginning she sends the players off together to do a review and diagnosis of the game without the coaches' input. While the players meet, Pat hears her coaches' observations. After about ten minutes, all coaches and players get together. The players share their findings and planned corrections, and Pat and the other coaches add their input as needed.

Pat also employs shared thinking during a time-out. For the first fifteen seconds, she hears from her assistant coaches. And then she talks to the players, asking for their input. Pat recalls that during a game against Vanderbilt, while she was talking with her assistants, Chamique Holdsclaw, who was only a freshman at the time, tugged on Pat's sleeve and interrupted her to say, "Give me the ball. Give me the *ball*." Pat gave her the ball, Holdsclaw scored, and the team won.[2]

APPLYING THE CASE STUDY

As you reflect on the story of Pat Summitt, think about the following:

1. Given some of your experiences with coaches, or given what you may have read about highly successful coaches, did it surprise you to read that Pat Summitt asks for so much input from her players and assistant coaches? Explain.

   _____

   _____

   _____

2. Why do you think Coach Summitt asks her players to get together without the coaches to diagnose what's going on in the game? What would change if she brought everyone together from the beginning? What would happen if she as the leader spoke first?

   _____

   _____

   _____

3. Do you think there comes a time in the life of a leader or an expert when shared thinking is no longer needed or desired? If so, why? If not, why not?

   _____

   _____

   _____

4. What qualities does Coach Summitt exhibit that encourage shared thinking? What other qualities are needed in a leader for shared thinking to be practiced? Does your leader possess those qualities? Do you possess those qualities?

   _____

   _____

   _____

HOW SHARED THINKING CAN MAKE YOU MORE SUCCESSFUL

Good thinkers, especially those who are also good leaders, understand the power of shared thinking. They know that when they value the thoughts and ideas of others, they receive the compounding results of shared thinking and accomplish more than they ever could on their own.

Those who participate in shared thinking understand the following:

1. Shared Thinking Is Faster than Solo Thinking

We live in a truly fast-paced world. To function at its current rate of speed, we can't go it alone. I think the generation of young men and women just entering the workforce sense that very strongly. Perhaps that is why they value community so highly and are more likely to work for a company they like than one that only pays them well.

Working with others is like giving yourself a shortcut. It helps everyone accomplish work more quickly. If you want to learn a new skill quickly, how do you do it? Do you go off by yourself and figure it out, or do you get someone to show you how? You can always learn more quickly from someone with experience—whether you're trying to learn how to use a new software package, develop your golf swing, or cook a new dish.

Do you naturally engage the assistance of others? Or do you tend to go it alone? How does your natural bent work for or against you?

_____

_____

_____

2. Shared Thinking Is More Innovative than Solo Thinking

We tend to think of great thinkers and innovators as soloists, but the truth is that the greatest innovative thinking doesn't occur in a vacuum. Innovation results from collaboration. Albert Einstein once remarked, "Many times a day I realize how much my own outer and inner life is built upon the labors of my fellow men, both living and dead, and how earnestly I must exert myself in order to give in return as much as I have received."

Shared thinking leads to greater innovation, whether you look at the work of researchers Marie and Pierre Curie, surrealists Luis Buñuel and Salvador Dalí, or songwriters John Lennon and Paul McCartney. If you combine your thoughts with the thoughts of others, you will come up with thoughts you've never had!

Where do you ordinarily look for inspiration and new ideas? Do you gaze inward or look outward? Do you try to spring-board off of others' ideas—whether through conversation or by reading books? Or do you try to invent on your own? How can you learn to engage more with others?

_____

_____

_____

3. Shared Thinking Brings More Maturity than Solo Thinking

As much as we would like to think that we know it all, each of us has blind spots and areas of inexperience. When I first started out as a pastor, I had many dreams and lots of energy, but I possessed little experience. To try to overcome that, I attempted to get several high-profile pastors of growing churches to share their thinking with me. In the early 1970s, I wrote letters to the ten most success-ful pastors in the country, offering them what was a huge amount of money to me at the time ($100) to meet me for an hour so that I could ask them questions. When one said yes, I'd visit him. I didn't talk much, except to ask a few questions. I wasn't there to impress anyone or satisfy my ego. I was there to learn. I listened to every-thing he said, took careful notes, and absorbed everything I could. Those experiences changed my life.

You've had experiences I haven't, and I've had experiences you haven't. Put us together and we bring a broader range of personal history—and therefore maturity—to the table. If you don't have the experience you need, meet up with someone who does.

How would you judge your level of experience? Do you possess it in abundance? Or do your dreams or energy far outweigh your wisdom? Who can you talk to in order to diminish your maturity gap? What specifically would you want them to help you with?

_____

_____

_____

4. Shared Thinking Is Stronger than Solo Thinking

Philosopher-poet Johann Wolfgang von Goethe said, "To accept good advice is but to increase one's own ability." Two heads are better than one — when they are thinking in the same direction.

Thinking together is like harnessing two horses to pull a wagon. They are stronger together than individually. Did you know that? Together they can move more weight than the sum of their best individual efforts. A synergy comes from working together. That same kind of energy comes into play when people think together.

Who have you worked well with in the past? Who have you experienced breakthroughs with? What was it about those people that help you be more effective?

_____

_____

_____

5. Shared Thinking Returns Greater Value than Solo Thinking

Because shared thinking is stronger than solo thinking, it's obvious that it yields a higher return. That happens because of the compounding action of shared thinking. But it also offers other benefits. The personal return you receive from shared thinking and experiences can be great.

Business executive Clarence Francis summed up the benefits in the following observation: "I sincerely believe that the word *relationships* is the key to the prospect of a decent world. It seems abundantly clear that every problem you will have — in your family, in your work, in our nation, or in this world—is essentially a matter of relationships, of interdependence."

Even the most introverted individuals benefit from being with the right people. List the benefits you receive when you spend time with people you enjoy.

_____

_____

_____

6. Shared Thinking Is the Only Way to Have Great Thinking

I believe that every great idea begins with three or four good ideas. And most good ideas come from shared thinking. Playwright Ben Jonson said, "He that is taught only by himself has a fool for a master."

When I was in school, teachers put the emphasis on being right and on doing better than the other students, rarely on working together to come up with good answers. Yet all the answers improve when they make the best use of everyone's thinking. If we each have one thought, and together we have two thoughts, then we always have the potential for a great thoughts.

Can you think of a single great idea you've ever had that was entirely your idea—with no contribution from any other person? If you do research, can you find a single great idea from any person that did not benefit from input from others? Give it a try. I believe if you dig deeply enough, you will find that other people's ideas always come into play.

_____

_____

_____

WHAT IF YOU BECAME BETTER AT
SHARED THINKING?

We can only grow in areas where we acknowledge that we need to improve. Think very honestly about yourself when it comes to shared thinking. How much do you need to improve in this area? What might change in your life if you were to start thinking collaboratively? How would that impact you professionally? Relationally? Financially? Spiritually? Spend some time reflecting and recording your thoughts here.

_____

_____

_____

_____

_____

_____

_____

_____

_____

_____

_____

_____

_____

_____

_____

_____

_____

_____

_____

HOW TO BECOME A SHARED THINKER

Some people naturally participate in shared thinking. Any time they see a problem, they think, *Who do I know who can help with this?* Leaders tend to be that way. So do extroverts. However, you don't have to be either of those to benefit from shared thinking. Use the following steps to help you improve your ability to harness shared thinking.

1. Value the Ideas of Others

First, believe that the ideas of other people have value. If you don't, your hands will be tied. How do you know if you truly want input from others? Ask yourself these questions:

- **Am I emotionally secure?** People who lack confidence and worry about their status, position, or power tend to reject the ideas of others, protect their turf, and keep people at bay. It takes a secure person to consider others' ideas.
- **Do I place value on people?** You won't value the ideas of a person if you don't value and respect people. Have you ever considered your conduct around people you value versus those you don't? Look at the differences:

If I Value People	If I Don't Value People
I want to spend time with them	I don't want to be around them
I listen to them	I neglect to listen
I want to help them	I don't offer them help
I am influenced by them	I ignore them
I respect them	I am indifferent

- **Do I value the interactive process?** A wonderful synergy often occurs as the result of shared thinking. It can take you places you've never been. Publisher Malcolm Forbes asserted, "Listening to advice often accomplishes far more than heeding it."

You must open yourself up to the *idea* of sharing ideas before you will engage in the *process* of shared thinking.

2. Move from Competition to Cooperation

Jeffrey J. Fox, author of *How to Become CEO,* says, "Always be on the lookout for ideas. Be completely indiscriminate as to the source. Get ideas from customers, children, competitors, other industries, or cab drivers. It doesn't matter who thought of an idea."[3]

A person who values cooperation desires to complete the ideas of others, not compete with them. If someone asks you to share ideas, focus on helping the team, not getting ahead personally. And if you are the one who brings people together to share their thoughts, praise the idea more than the source of the idea. If the best idea always wins, then all will share their thoughts with greater enthusiasm.

3. Have an Agenda When You Meet

I enjoy spending time with certain people, whether we discuss ideas or not: my wife, Margaret; my children; my grandchildren; my parents. Though we often do discuss ideas, it doesn't bother me if we don't; we are family. When I spend time with nearly anyone else in my life, however, I have an agenda. I know what I want to accomplish.

The more I respect the wisdom of the person, the more I listen. For example, when I meet with someone I'm mentoring, I let the person ask the questions, but I expect to do most of the talking. When I meet with someone who mentors me, I mostly keep my mouth shut. In other relationships, the give-and-take is more even. But no matter what, I have a reason for getting together and I have an expectation for what I'll give to it and get from it. That's true whether it's for business or pleasure.

4. Get the Right People Around the Table

To get anything of value out of shared thinking, you need to have people *around* the table who bring something *to* the table. As you prepare to ask people to participate in shared thinking, use the following criteria for the selection process. Choose:

- People whose greatest desire is the success of the ideas
- People who can add value to one another's thoughts

- People who can emotionally handle quick changes in the conversation
- People who appreciate the strengths of others in areas where they themselves are weak
- People who understand their place of value at the table
- People who place what is best for the team before themselves
- People who can bring out the best thinking in the people around them
- People who possess maturity, experience, and success in the issue under discussion
- People who will take ownership and responsibility for decisions
- People who will leave the table with a "we" attitude, not a "me" attitude

Too often we choose our brainstorming partners based on feelings of friendship or circumstances or convenience. But that doesn't help us to discover and create the ideas of the highest order. Who we invite to the table makes all the difference.

5. Compensate Good Thinkers and Collaborators Well

Successful organizations practice shared thinking. If you lead an organization, department, or team, then you can't afford to be without people who are good at shared thinking. As you recruit and hire, look for good thinkers who value others, have experience with the collaborative process, and are emotionally secure. Then pay them well and challenge them to use their thinking skills and share their ideas often. Nothing adds value like a lot of good thinkers putting their minds together.

SHARED THINKING ACTION PLAN

1. **Check Your Attitude:** For each of the following statements, rate yourself on a scale of 1 to 10 (with 10 meaning 100 percent agreement):

   I like people and always place a high value on them.

   1 2 3 4 5 6 7 8 9 10

   I value other people's opinions as much as my own.

   1 2 3 4 5 6 7 8 9 10

   I do not feel threatened by the success of my employees.

   1 2 3 4 5 6 7 8 9 10

   I do not feel jealous when a coworker receives recognition.

   1 2 3 4 5 6 7 8 9 10

   I do not feel threatened or challenged when others' ideas are better than mine.

   1 2 3 4 5 6 7 8 9 10

   If you scored anything lower than an 8 in any of these, then your attitude may be hindering your ability to engage in shared thinking. Do some soul searching to discover how you can develop a more open attitude toward collaboration.

2. **Find a Thinking Partner:** Some of the greatest stories of invention, innovation, and creativity have come as the result of partnerships. Think about the people you know. Can you identify someone with similar hopes and dreams whom you admire and with whom you have great chemistry? If so, that person may be a candidate for creative partnership. Explore the concept of shared thinking with this person to see what potential it has.

3. **Look at Your Current Team:** Some of the challenges you are currently facing would benefit greatly from shared thinking. Think about the people currently working on your team or in your area. List their names. Then use the following checklist to determine how well they work in a shared thinking environment:

A. Does he/she desire the success of an idea at least as much as personal credit?

B. Can he/she add value to another person's ideas?

C. Can he/she emotionally handle quick changes in the conversation?

D. Does he/she understand his/her strengths and value to the team?

E. Will he/she place what is best for the team before him-/herself?

F. Does he/she usually bring out the best thinking in others?

G. Does he/she possess maturity, experience, and success?

H. Will he/she take ownership and responsibility for decisions?

I. Will he/she leave the table with a "we" attitude, not a "me" attitude?

Name	A	B	C	D	E	F	G	H	I

Any person for whom you have many yes answers is a good candidate to participate in shared thinking to advance the team or organization. Anyone for whom you answer no too often or no for critical questions is likely to cause more harm than good and should not be invited into the process.

4. **Develop an Agenda:** If you are naturally relational, you may have a tendency to get together with other people and do nothing more than enjoy their company. There's nothing wrong with doing that with some people, but if you want to benefit from shared thinking, you must become more strategic in certain situations.

   Review your calendar for the coming week. Examine every appointment or activity you have listed. Which of them could be taken to the next level through the use of shared thinking? Which would benefit both you and the other people involved if you were to engage in shared thinking? Create an agenda for each of them. Take some time to clarify what you want to get out of an interaction with each person and what you expect to give. Write down questions or ideas to bring into the time you have together. You may be surprised by how much more productive your time will become.

AN EXERCISE IN SHARED THINKING

They say two heads are better than one. Name some of the people whose partnership has made your thinking better.

_____

_____

_____

_____

_____

What specific ideas have these people helped you create?

_____

_____

_____

_____

_____

How can you show appreciation to them this week for their partnership?

_____

_____

_____

Is there a person listed above, or someone you haven't included, who may be able to help you work through a problem you're currently facing? Or perhaps you are in a position to help one of the people above with an issue he or she is struggling with. Schedule time to meet with that person.

DISCUSSION QUESTIONS

1. Name a partnership or team of writers, artists, scientists, inventors, or businesspeople you greatly admire for their creativity. What work of theirs do you most admire? What made them so good?
2. What are the factors that come into play on an effective team?
3. What role does shared thinking play on effective teams? Is it possible to have a winning team when people don't share ideas? Explain.
4. Describe a time when you participated in a fantastic team or group activity. What made it so enjoyable to you?
5. In general, do you normally work better alone or in groups? Why?
6. What does a leader have to do to win people over to participating in shared thinking?
7. When it comes to contributing to brainstorming sessions, discussions, and other shared-thinking activities, what is your greatest strength? What is your greatest weakness? What do you do to keep yourself contributing where you're strong and staying out of the way where you're weak?
8. What would you like to see happen related to shared thinking on your current team or in your working environment?

10

Practice Unselfish Thinking

We cannot hold a torch to light another's path without brightening our own.

— Ben Sweetland

So far in this book, we've discussed many kinds of thinking that can help you to achieve more. Each of them has the potential to make you more successful. Now I want to acquaint you with a kind of thinking that has the potential to change your life in another way. It might even redefine how you view success.

I believe that no person can be successful in this life without helping other people. It doesn't matter how rich he becomes, how famous, how admired or respected. Awards and rewards count for little, if the only living a person has done is for himself.

Where do you stand when it comes to unselfish thinking? Do you believe you've been put on this earth to help others or merely yourself? Not sure of your motives? Then ask yourself two questions that Benjamin Franklin did every day. When he got up in the morning, he would ask, "What good am I going to do today?" And before he went to bed, he would ask, "What good have I done today?" If you can with integrity answer those questions with specifics on a regular basis, then you're headed in the right direction. And you can make a positive difference in this world.

UNSELFISH THINKING CASE STUDY

In 1885, a young man named George used every penny he had to travel to Highland College in Highland, Kansas. Getting an education had been his driving goal since he was a boy, walking nine miles each way to school and leaving home for good at age twelve to attend high school. However, on the day he got to Highland College, his hopes were dashed. Even though his application had already been accepted, when school officials discovered that he was black, they turned him away.

For a few years, George tried to establish a homestead. He had a knack for growing things, but his desire to continue his education was too strong. In 1890, he once again attempted to enroll in school, and he was accepted by Simpson College, which accepted students regardless of race.

By all accounts, George excelled in the arts. But in 1891 when he transferred to Iowa State, he changed his major from art to agriculture. Why? James Wilson, who was the dean of Agriculture at Iowa State, recalled the reason in this statement addressed to George:

> I remember when I first met you, you said you wanted to get an agricultural education so you could help your race. I had never known anything more beautiful than that said by a student. I know the taste you have for painting and the success you have made along that line, and I said, 'Why not push your studies along that line to some extent?' When you replied that that would be of no value to your colored brethren, that also was magnificent.[1]

George summed up his change in studies simply by saying, art "would not do [my] people as much good."[2]

George Washington Carver went on to receive degrees in agriculture, botany, and horticulture from Iowa State. Then he became the first African American faculty member at Iowa State College.

In April 1896, Carver received an unusual offer from Dr. Booker T. Washington of the Tuskegee Institute: to teach and become the school's director of agriculture. Washington said,

I cannot offer you money, position, or fame. The first two you have. The last, from the position you now occupy, you will no doubt achieve. These things I now ask you to give up. I offer you in their place: work...hard, hard work, the task of bringing a people from degradation, poverty, and waste to full manhood. Your department exists only on paper and your laboratory will have to be in your head.[3]

Carver could have lived a comfortable life in Iowa. Yet he gave it up to move to Alabama, in the heart of the Deep South, where he would be regarded as a second-class citizen.

While at Tuskegee Institute, Carver earned the respect of such innovators as Thomas Edison and Henry Ford. His agricultural research and discoveries improved farming throughout the country, and he was especially successful helping the poor black farmers of the South. And he accomplished all that he did with minimal resources or support.

If Carver had focused on patenting his findings or building a business based on his discoveries, he could have been a very rich man. But that wasn't his goal. Carver explained his philosophy this way: "It is not the style of clothes one wears, neither the kind of automobile one drives, nor the amount of money one has in the bank, that counts. These mean nothing. It is simply service that measures success." What George Washington Carver found was more than success. By thinking beyond himself, he discovered significance.

APPLYING THE CASE STUDY

Consider the case of George Washington Carver and answer the following questions:

1. What motivated George Washington Carver to dedicate his life to agriculture? Do you think his was a worthy goal? Explain.

   _____

   _____

   _____

2. Do you agree that Carver's decision to give up art was the right one? What might he have done with other fields to help other people? Do you think it could have contributed more than agriculture? If so, how?

   _____

   _____

   _____

3. How difficult would it have been for you to give up the study of something you love and have talent for in order to pursue another goal that you thought would benefit others more?

   _____

   _____

   _____

4. What are your greatest talents? Name two to five. Which of them has the greatest potential to benefit others? How has that ability come into play in your goals, dreams, and career choices?

   _____

   _____

   _____

HOW UNSELFISH THINKING CAN
MAKE YOU MORE SUCCESSFUL

Unselfish thinking can often deliver a return greater than any other kind of thinking. Take a look at some of its benefits:

1. Unselfish Thinking Brings Personal Fulfillment

Few things in life bring greater personal rewards than helping others. Charles H. Burr believed, "Getters generally don't get happiness; givers get it." Helping people brings great satisfaction. When you spend your day unselfishly serving others, at night you can lay down your head and sleep soundly with few regrets.

Even if you have spent much of your life pursuing selfish gain, it's never too late to have a change of heart. That's what Alfred Nobel did. When he saw his own obituary mistakenly printed in the newspaper (his brother had died and the editor had written about the wrong Nobel, saying that the explosives his company produced had killed many people), Nobel vowed to promote peace and acknowledge contributions to humanity. That is how the Nobel Prizes came into being.

What kinds of unselfish pursuits give you personal satisfaction? How much of your time, energy, and resources are you currently putting into those pursuits?

_____

_____

_____

2. Unselfish Thinking Adds Value to Others

In 1904, Bessie Anderson Stanley wrote the following definition of success in *Brown Book* magazine:

He has achieved success who has lived well, laughed often and loved much; who has enjoyed the trust of pure women, the respect of intelligent men and the love of little children; who has filled his niche and accomplished his task; who has left the world better than he found it, whether by an improved poppy, a

perfect poem, or a rescued soul; who has never lacked appreciation of Earth's beauty or failed to express it; who has always
looked for the best in others and given them the best he had;
whose life was an inspiration; whose memory a benediction.

When you get outside of yourself and make a contribution to
others, you really begin to live.

*How do you add value to other people on a consistent basis? If
you don't on a consistent basis, then think of one specific time
you did. Describe it.*

_____

_____

_____

3. Unselfish Thinking Encourages Other Virtues

Of all the qualities a person can pursue, unselfish thinking
seems to make the biggest difference toward cultivating other virtues. I think that's because the ability to give unselfishly is so difficult. It goes against the grain of human nature. But if you can learn
to think unselfishly and become a giver, then it becomes easier to
develop many other virtues: gratitude, love, respect, patience, discipline, etc.

*What small actions can you take immediately to help you
encourage other virtues?*

_____

_____

_____

4. Unselfish Thinking Increases Quality of Life

The spirit of generosity created by unselfish thinking gives
people an appreciation for life and an understanding of its higher
values. Seeing those in need and giving to meet those needs puts a
lot of things into perspective. It increases the quality of the life of
the giver and of the receiver. That's why I believe:

There is no life as empty as the self-centered life.
There is no life as centered as the self-empty life.

If you want to improve your world, then focus your attention on helping others.

How would you describe your current quality of life? I don't mean necessarily financially, but mentally, emotionally, and spiritually? Do you feel it could be better? Explore the possibility that to improve it, you should perhaps seek to give more rather than get more.

_____

_____

_____

5. Unselfish Thinking Makes You Part of Something Greater than Yourself

Merck and Company, the global pharmaceutical corporation, has always seen itself as doing more than just producing products and making a profit. It desires to serve humanity. In the mid-1980s, the company developed a drug to cure river blindness, a disease that infects and causes blindness in millions of people, particularly in developing countries. They did this in spite of the fact that potential customers couldn't afford to buy it. Instead, Merck simply announced that it would give the medicine free to anyone who needed it. As of 1998, the company had given more than 250 million tablets away.[4]

George W. Merck says, "We try never to forget that medicine is for the people. It is not for the profits. The profits follow, and if we have remembered that, they have never failed to appear." The lesson to be learned? Simple. Instead of trying to be great, be part of something greater than yourself.

What cause, mission, or purpose greater than yourself are you truly part of? What is the evidence of your participation? If you are unable to give an answer, then consider what you would like to be a part of. To contribute on a higher level, you need to be part of something great you believe in.

_____

_____

_____

6. Unselfish Thinking Creates a Legacy

Jack Balousek, president and chief operating officer of True North Communications, says, "Learn, earn, return—these are the three phases of life. The first third should be devoted to education, the second third to building a career and making a living, and the last third to giving back to others—returning something in gratitude. Each state seems to be a preparation for the next one."

If you are successful, it becomes possible for you to leave an inheritance *for* others. But if you desire to do more, to create a legacy, then you need to leave that *in* others. When you think unselfishly and invest in others, you gain the opportunity to create a legacy that will outlive you.

What do you want your legacy to be? How do you want your epitaph to read? It's never too early to begin thinking about that.

_____

_____

_____

WHAT IF YOU BECAME BETTER
AT UNSELFISH THINKING?

We can only change, grow, and improve in areas where we acknowledge that we need to improve. Think very honestly about yourself when it comes to unselfish thinking? How much do you need to improve in this area? What might change in your life if you were to start thinking unselfishly? How would that impact you professionally? Relationally? Financially? Spiritually? Spend some time reflecting and recording your thoughts here.

HOW TO BECOME AN UNSELFISH THINKER

I think most people recognize the value of unselfish thinking, and most would even agree that it's an ability they would like to develop. Many people, however, are at a loss concerning how to change their thinking. To begin cultivating the ability to think unselfishly, I recommend that you do the following:

1. Put Others First

The process begins with realizing that everything is not about you! That requires humility and a shift in focus. In *The Power of Ethical Management,* Ken Blanchard and Norman Vincent Peale wrote, "People with humility don't think less of themselves... they just think about themselves less."

If you want to become less selfish in your thinking, then you need to stop thinking about your wants and begin focusing on others' needs. Paul the Apostle exhorted, "Do nothing out of selfish ambition or vain conceit, but in humility consider others better than yourselves. Each of you should look not only to your own interests, but also to the interests of others."[5] Make a mental and emotional commitment to look out for the interests of others.

2. Expose Yourself to Situations Where People Have Needs

It's one thing to believe you are willing to give unselfishly. It's another to actually do it. To make the transition, you need to put yourself in a position where you can see people's needs and do something about it.

The kind of giving you do isn't important at first. You can serve at your church, make donations to a food bank, volunteer professional services, or give to a charitable organization. The point is to learn how to give and to cultivate the habit of thinking like a giver.

3. Give Quietly or Anonymously

It's almost always easier to give when you receive recognition for it than it is when no one is likely to know about it. The people who give in order to receive a lot of fanfare, however, have already received any reward they will get. There are spiritual, mental, and emotional benefits that come only to those who give anonymously. If you've never done it before, try it.

4. Invest in People Intentionally

If you want to become the kind of person who invests in people, then consider others and their journey so that you can collaborate with them. As you go into any relationship, think about how you can invest in the other person so that it becomes a win-win situation. Here is how relationships most often play out:

I win, you lose — I win only once.
You win, I lose — you win only once.
We both win — we win many times.
We both lose — good-bye, partnership!

The best relationships are win-win. Why don't more people go into relationships with that attitude? I'll tell you why: most people want to make sure that they win first. Unselfish thinkers, on the other hand, go into a relationship and make sure that the other person wins first. And that makes all the difference.

5. Continually Check Your Motives

François de la Rochefoucauld said, "What seems to be generosity is often no more than disguised ambition, which overlooks a small interest in order to secure a great one." The hardest thing for most people is fighting their natural tendency to put themselves first. That's why it's important to continually examine your motives to make sure you're not sliding backward into selfishness.

UNSELFISH THINKING ACTION PLAN

1. **Set Unselfish Goals:** How many of your goals are unselfish? How many are focused entirely on others?

   Think about some things you could do to help others that will in no way benefit you (other than to give you internal satisfaction). Set an amount of money to give away this year. Decide how many hours a week or month you will dedicate to serving others. Find something you believe in that you can help to succeed—not necessarily by trying to run it, but by simply assisting wherever you are asked to. If you set unselfish goals and look for ways to meet them, you will begin to think more unselfishly.

2. **Give from Your Best:** An investment in a person ultimately pays the highest return because it can result in changed lives. Think about what you have to invest in another person. What skills do you possess that someone would benefit from learning? What life experiences have you had that can help another person? What resources do you possess that ought to be shared? Once you have figured out what you have to give, then look for people with potential who would be glad to receive it, and start investing.

3. **Make Your Agreements Win-Win:** The next time you put together a deal or develop a professional relationship, think in terms of win-win. If neither you nor the other person would benefit, then don't go through with it. And once you've determined that it will be good for both of you, make the effort to guarantee that the other person wins first.

4. **Give Anonymously:** Find something you believe in and then give to it without anyone (except your spouse, if you're married) knowing about it. Then do it again. Make it a regular practice. You will be amazed by how it can change your attitude.

AN EXERCISE IN UNSELFISH THINKING

Starting today and for the next seven days, write in the answers to the questions below.

Day 1
Morning: "What good am I going to do today?"

_____

_____

_____

Evening: "What good have I done today?"

_____

_____

_____

Day 2
Morning: "What good am I going to do today?"

_____

_____

_____

Evening: "What good have I done today?"

_____

_____

_____

Day 3
Morning: "What good am I going to do today?"

_____

_____

_____

Evening: "What good have I done today?"

_____

_____

_____

Day 4

Morning: "What good am I going to do today?"

_____

_____

_____

Evening: "What good have I done today?"

_____

_____

_____

Day 5

Morning: "What good am I going to do today?"

_____

_____

_____

Evening: "What good have I done today?"

_____

_____

_____

Day 6

Morning: "What good am I going to do today?"

_____

_____

_____

Evening: "What good have I done today?"

_____

_____

_____

Day 7
Morning: "What good am I going to do today?"

_____

_____

_____

Evening: "What good have I done today?"

_____

_____

_____

DISCUSSION QUESTIONS

1. What's it like to be around selfish people? To be around unselfish people? What kind of reaction does each kind of person cause in you?
2. Who is the most unselfish person you've ever met? Describe him or her.
3. Describe a win-win situation or deal that you have been a part of. Who initiated it? Did you expect it to be mutually beneficial when you started? What happened as a result?
4. How risky do you believe it would be to enter an agreement guaranteeing that the other person or party would win first? Would you be hesitant to do such a thing? Explain.
5. What kinds of things do you do to curb any natural selfishness you may have? How well do they work?
6. How do you feel when you find yourself in situations with people who have needs? How do you usually respond? How would you like to respond if you could? What would have to happen for you to do what you would like?
7. What vision, cause, calling, or purpose greater than yourself do you believe in? What do you do or give to advance it? Why?
8. Who are you investing in on a regular basis? What are you doing with that person? How does it help him or her? Is that something you would like to do more of? If so, what must happen for you to do more of it?

Rely on Bottom-Line Thinking

There ain't no rules around here. We're trying to accomplish something.

— THOMAS EDISON

How do you figure out the bottom line for your organization, business, department, team, or group? In many businesses, the bottom line is literally the bottom line: profit determines whether you are succeeding. But dollars should not always be the primary measure of success. Would you measure the ultimate success of your family by how much money you had at the end of the month or year? And if you run a nonprofit or volunteer organization, how would you know whether you were performing at your highest potential? How do you think bottom line in that situation?

If you're accustomed to thinking of the bottom line only as it relates to financial matters, then you may be missing some things crucial to you and your organization. Instead, think of the bottom line as the end, the takeaway, the desired result. Every activity has its own unique bottom line. If you have a job, your work has a bottom line. If you serve in your church, your activity has a bottom line. So does your effort as a parent, or spouse, if you are one.

If you are engaged in activities and you never determine what your bottom line is, then you run the risk of having activity without accomplishment or any real sense of purpose.

BOTTOM-LINE THINKING CASE STUDY

Frances Hesselbein had to ask herself bottom-line questions in 1976, when she became the national executive director of the Girl Scouts of America. When she first got involved with the Girl Scouts, running the organization was the last thing she expected to do. She and her husband, John, were partners in Hesselbein Studios, a small family business that filmed television commercials and promotional films. She wrote the scripts and he made the films. In the early 1950s, she was recruited as a volunteer Girl Scout troop leader at the Second Presbyterian Church in Johnstown, Pennsylvania. Even that was unusual, since she had a son and no daughters. But she agreed to do it on a temporary basis. She must have loved it, because she led the troop for nine years!

In time, she became council president and a member of the national board. Then she served as executive director of the Talus Rock Girl Scout Council, a full-time paid position. By the time she took the job as CEO of the national organization, the Girl Scouts was in trouble. The organization lacked direction, teenage girls were losing interest in scouting, and it was becoming increasingly difficult to recruit adult volunteers, especially with greater numbers of women entering the workforce. Meanwhile, the Boy Scouts was considering opening itself to girls. Hesselbein desperately needed to bring the organization back to the bottom line.

"We kept asking ourselves very simple questions," she says. "What is our business? Who is our customer? And what does the customer consider value? If you're the Girl Scouts, IBM, or AT&T, you have to manage for a mission."[1] Hesselbein's focus on mission enabled her to identify the Girl Scouts' bottom line. "We really are here for one reason: to help a girl reach her highest potential. More than any one thing, that made the difference. Because when you are clear about your mission, corporate goals and operating objectives flow from it."[2]

Once she figured out her bottom line, she was able to create a strategy to achieve it. She started by reorganizing the national staff. Then she created a planning system to be used by each of the 350 regional councils. And she introduced management training to the organization.

Hesselbein didn't restrict herself to changes in leadership and organization. In the 1960s and '70s, the country had changed and so had its girls — but the Girl Scouts hadn't. Hesselbein tackled that issue, too. The organization made its activities more relevant to the current culture, giving greater opportunities for using computers, for example, rather than hosting a party. She also sought out minority participation, created bilingual materials, and reached out to low-income households. If helping girls reach their highest potential was the group's bottom line, then why not be more aggressive helping girls who traditionally have fewer opportunities? The strategy worked beautifully. Minority participation in the Girl Scouts tripled.

In 1990, Hesselbein left the Girl Scouts after making it a first-class organization. She went on to become the founding president and CEO of the Peter F. Drucker Foundation for Nonprofit Management and now serves as chairman of its board of governors. And in 1998, she was awarded the Presidential Medal of Freedom. President Bill Clinton said of Hesselbein during the ceremony at the White House, "She has shared her remarkable recipe for inclusion and excellence with countless organizations whose bottom line is measured not in dollars, but in changed lives."[3] He couldn't have said it better!

APPLYING THE CASE STUDY

As you reflect on the work of Frances Hesselbein, consider these questions:

1. How difficult do you think it was for Frances Hesselbein to identify the bottom line of the Girl Scouts at the time she took over the organization? Explain.

   _____

   _____

   _____

2. The Girl Scouts is a nonprofit organization. Do you think identifying the bottom line for a nonprofit is easier or more difficult than for a for-profit organization? Why?

   _____

   _____

   _____

3. How did bottom-line thinking impact the Girl Scouts? What do you think might have happened to the organization if a good bottom-line thinker had not been asked to lead it?

   _____

   _____

   _____

4. How should a leader balance purpose and profits in a business?

   _____

   _____

   _____

HOW BOTTOM-LINE THINKING CAN
MAKE YOU MORE SUCCESSFUL

As you explore the concept of bottom-line thinking, recognize that it can help you in many ways:

1. Bottom-Line Thinking Provides Great Clarity

What's the difference between bowling and work? When bowling, it takes only three seconds to know how you've done! That's one reason people love sports so much. There's no waiting and no guessing about the outcome.

Bottom-line thinking makes it possible for you to measure outcomes more quickly and easily. It gives you a benchmark by which to measure activity. It can be used as a focused way of ensuring that all your little activities are purposeful and line up to achieve a larger goal.

When you work, do you often think in terms of larger goals? Or are you usually focused on the task at hand? What could you do to keep the bottom line in mind?

_____

_____

_____

2. Bottom-Line Thinking Helps You Assess Every Situation

When you know your bottom line, it becomes much easier to know how you're doing in any given area. When Frances Hesselbein began running the Girl Scouts, for example, she measured everything against the organization's goal of helping a girl reach her highest potential—from the organization's management structure (which she changed from a hierarchy to a hub) down to what badges the girls could earn. There's no better measurement tool than the bottom line.

How do you measure results in your career? Does your boss use the same criteria you do? What about the organization? If there is inconsistency between the three, you may find it difficult to be successful.

_____

_____

_____

3. Bottom-Line Thinking Helps You Make the Best Decisions

Decisions become much easier when you know your bottom line. When the Girl Scouts were struggling in the 1970s, outside organizations tried to convince its members to become women's rights activists or door-to-door canvassers. But under Hesselbein, it became easy for the Girl Scouts to say no. It knew its bottom line, and it wanted to pursue its goals with focus and fervency.

What criteria do you use to make decisions in your career? With your family? In your spiritual life? For your finances?

_____

_____

_____

4. Bottom-Line Thinking Generates High Morale

When you know the bottom line and you go after it, you greatly increase your odds of winning. And nothing generates high morale like winning. How do you describe sports teams that win the championship, or company divisions that achieve their goals, or volunteers who achieve their mission? They're excited. Hitting the target feels exhilarating. And you can hit it only if you know what it is.

What gets you excited professionally?

_____

_____

_____

5. Bottom-Line Thinking Ensures Your Future

If you want to be successful tomorrow, you need to think bottom line today. That's what Frances Hesselbein did, and she turned the Girl Scouts around. Look at any successful, lasting company, and you'll find leaders who know their bottom line. They make their decisions, allocate their resources, hire their people, and structure their organization to achieve that bottom line.

Are all of your professional efforts in accord with you bottom line? If not, where are the misalignments? What can you do to put everything on the right track?

_____

_____

_____

WHAT IF YOU BECAME BETTER AT
BOTTOM-LINE THINKING?

We can only change, grow, and improve in areas where we acknowledge that we need to improve. Think very honestly about yourself when it comes to bottom-line thinking. How much do you need to improve in this area? What might change in your life if you were to start thinking in a more bottom-line manner? How would that impact you professionally? Relationally? Financially? Spiritually? Spend some time reflecting and recording your thoughts here.

_____

_____

_____

_____

_____

_____

_____

_____

_____

_____

_____

_____

_____

_____

_____

_____

_____

HOW TO BECOME A BOTTOM-LINE THINKER

I don't think it's hard to see the value of the bottom line. Most people would agree that bottom-line thinking has a high return. But learning how to be a bottom-line thinker can be challenging. Here are some tips to help you:

1. Identify the Real Bottom Line

The process of bottom-line thinking begins with knowing what you're really going after. It can be as lofty as the big-picture vision, mission, or purpose of an organization. Or it can be as focused as what you want to accomplish on a particular project. What's important is that you be as specific as possible. If your goal is for something as vague as "success," you will have a painfully difficult time trying to harness bottom-line thinking to achieve it.

The first step is to set aside your "wants." Get to the results you're really looking for, the true essence of the goal. Set aside any emotions that may cloud your judgment and remove any politics that may influence your perception. What are you really trying to achieve? When you strip away all the things that don't really matter, what are you compelled to achieve? What must occur? What is acceptable? That is the real bottom line.

2. Make the Bottom Line the Point

Have you ever been in a conversation with someone whose intentions seem other than stated? Sometimes the situation reflects intentional deception. But it can also occur when the person doesn't know his own bottom line.

The same thing happens in companies. Sometimes, for example, an idealistically stated mission and the real bottom line don't jibe. Purpose and profits compete. Earlier, I quoted George W. Merck, who stated, "We try never to forget that medicine is for the people. It is not for the profits. The profits follow, and if we have remembered that, they have never failed to appear." He probably made that statement to remind those in his organization that profits *serve* purpose — they don't compete with it.

If making a profit were the real bottom line, and helping people merely provided the means for achieving it, then the company would suffer. Its attention would be divided, and it would neither help people as well as it could nor make as much profit as it desired.

3. Create a Strategic Plan to Achieve the Bottom Line

Once the bottom line has been determined, a strategy must be created to achieve it. In organizations, that often means identifying the core elements or functions that must operate properly to achieve the bottom line. This is the leader's responsibility.

The important thing is that when the bottom line of each activity is achieved, then *the* bottom line is achieved. If the sum of the smaller goals doesn't add up to the real bottom line, then either your strategy is flawed or you've not identified your real bottom line.

4. Align Team Members with the Bottom Line

Once you have your strategy in place, make sure your people line up with your strategy. Ideally, all team members should know the big goal, as well as their individual roles in achieving it. They need to know their personal bottom lines and how they work to achieve the organization's bottom line.

5. Stick with One System and Monitor Results Continually

My friend Dave Sutherland believes that some organizations get into trouble by trying to mix systems. He maintains that many kinds of systems can be successful, but mixing different systems or continually changing from one to another leads to failure. Dave says,

> Bottom-line thinking cannot be a one-time thing. It has to be built into the system of working and relating and achieving. You can't just tune into the desired result every now and then. Achieving with bottom-line thinking must be a way of life, or it will send conflicting messages. I am a bottom-line thinker. It is a part of my "system" for achievement. I practice it every day. No other measurements — no wasted efforts.

Dave calls members of his field team every night to ask about the bottom line. He continually keeps his eye on the company's bottom line by monitoring it for every core area.

BOTTOM-LINE THINKING ACTION PLAN

1. **Define the Bottom Line:** How much have you thought about your own bottom line? Do you know why you're doing what you're doing in your career? Have you figured out what you're trying to accomplish in your family life? If someone asked, would you be able to tell him for what purpose you've been put on this earth?

   Your life can be more fulfilling and your thinking can be more fruitful if you know your purpose. Give some thought to each of the following areas. Then try to write succinctly what your bottom line is for each. (You may want to add additional areas not listed below.)

   Career:
   Marriage:
   Parenting:
   Recreation:
   Service:
   Spiritual Life:
   Purpose:

   Don't feel bad if you don't have perfect clarity on all of these issues. It takes most people years to figure it all out. This exercise is merely a starting point.

2. **Align as Many Areas As You Can:** There is great power in aligning the various areas in your life. At the very least, your bottom-line principles cannot contradict one another. But it's even better if the various areas work together toward common, compatible goals.

   Examine what you wrote in the previous exercise to look for conflicts or contradictions. Try to reconcile all that you can. And then put them in order of importance so that you have a sense of the priorities of your life.

3. **Incorporate the Bottom Line into Your Thinking:** Once you have begun to identify the bottom line in the various areas of your life, you need to incorporate those touch points

into your thinking. Write them down and place them where you will see them while you are engaged in those parts of your life. Make them a filter for everything you do. Continually ask yourself, "Is what I'm doing adding to the bottom line in this area? Or is what I'm doing nonessential?" You should make it your goal to eliminate things from your life that don't contribute.

4. **Align Your Team:** If you are the leader of a team, a department, or an organization, it is your responsibility to communicate the bottom line to your people and organize their efforts toward achieving that bottom line. Change structure, organization, incentives, job descriptions, budgets, etc., so that everything and everyone is in alignment with the bottom line. And continue communicating the vision and checking to make sure everything stays aligned.

AN EXERCISE IN BOTTOM-LINE THINKING

Have you ever been in a work situation where the bottom line was unclear? Explain.

_____

_____

_____

_____

How did this affect how specific tasks were done?

_____

_____

_____

_____

What one thing could the leader(s) have done differently to clarify the bottom line?

_____

_____

_____

_____

DISCUSSION QUESTIONS

1. Does the concept of bottom-line thinking seem more prag-
   matic or more idealistic to you?
2. Do you think profitability is a worthwhile bottom line for a
   business? Or do you think it's better to see profit as a result of
   a more philosophical bottom line? Why?
3. How do focusing on a bottom line and creating an environment in a workplace impact one another? Do they go hand in
   hand, or are they often at cross-purposes? Explain.
4. Is there a stated bottom line where you work? If so, what is it?
   Is that stated purpose or bottom line consistent with what
   you've observed as far as the values, structure, and leadership
   of the organization? Explain.
5. What does your organization use as a scoreboard? Does it
   encourage the right things? Can you think of a better one?
6. Do you tend to be a pragmatist or an idealist? How does your
   personality impact you when it comes to bottom-line thinking? How would you like to improve?
7. In what area of your life do you most often use bottom-line
   thinking? In what area do you utilize it the least? How might
   employing it in that area help you?
8. Have you identified a personal bottom line for yourself—an
   overarching purpose for living? If so, what is it? How does it
   help you?

NOTES

Introduction

1. Jim Collins and Jerry I. Porras, *Built to Last: Successful Habits of Visionary Companies* (New York: HarperBusiness, 1994), 213.

Chapter 2. Engage in Focused Thinking

1. Annette Moser-Wellman, *The Five Faces of Genius: The Skills to Master Ideas at Work* (New York: Viking, 2001), 111.
2. Al Ries, *Focus: The Future of Your Company Depends on It* (New York: HarperBusiness, 1996), 1.
3. M. Scott Peck, *The Road Less Traveled* (New York: Simon and Schuster, 1978), 27–28.

Chapter 3. Harness Creative Thinking

1. Moser-Wellman, *Five Faces of Genius,* 9. (Italics in the original.)
2. Cheryl Dahle, "Mind Games," *Fast Company,* January–February 2000, 170.
3. Ernie J. Zelinski, *The Joy of Not Knowing It All: Profiting from Creativity at Work or Play* (Chicago: VIP Books, 1994), 7.

Chapter 4. Employ Realistic Thinking

1. Chris Palochko, "Security a Huge Issue at Super Bowl," February 2, 2002, http://sports.yahoo.com/nfl/news (article no longer available).
2. James Allen, *As a Man Thinketh,* in *The Wisdom of James Allen* (San Diego: Laurel Creek Press, 1997).

Chapter 5. Utilize Strategic Thinking

1. Terry Ryan, *The Prize Winner of Defiance, Ohio: How My Mother Raised 10 Kids on 25 Words or Less* (New York: Touchstone, 2001), 25. (Italics in the original.)
2. Ibid., 92. (Italics in the original.)
3. Bobb Biehl, *Masterplanning: A Complete Guide for Building a Strategic Plan for Your Business, Church, or Organization* (Nashville: Broadman and Holman, 1997), 10.

Chapter 6. Explore Possibility Thinking

1. Thomas G. Smith, *Industrial Light & Magic: The Art of Special Effects* (New York: Ballantine Books, 1986), 9–10.
2. Chris Salewicz, *George Lucas* (New York: Thunders' Mouth Press, 1998), 105.
3. Richard Corliss, "Ready, Set, Glow!" *Time,* April 26, 1999.
4. Salewicz, *George Lucas*, 113.
5. Sally Kline, ed., *George Lucas: Interviews* (Jackson: University Press of Mississippi, 1999), 96.
6. "Leadership Lessons: An Interview with Don Soderquist," Willow Creek Association.

Chapter 7. Learn from Reflective Thinking

1. Mark Twain, *Following the Equator* (Hopewell, NJ: Ecco Press, 1996), 96.

Chapter 8. Question Popular Thinking

1. Alice Park, "Heart Mender," *Time,* August 20, 2001, 36.
2. Benno Müller-Hill, "Science, Truth, and Other Values," *Quarterly Review of Biology* 68, no. 3 (September 1993), 399–407.

Chapter 9. Benefit from Shared Thinking

1. Pat Summitt with Sally Jenkins, *Reach for the Summit* (New York: Broadway Books, 1998), 258.

2. Ibid., 69.

3. Jeffrey J. Fox, *How to Become CEO: The Rules for Rising to the Top of Any Organization* (New York: Hyperion, 1998), 115.

Chapter 10. Practice Unselfish Thinking

1. Peter Duncan Burchard, "George Washington Carver in Iowa: Preparation for Life Serving Humanity," *Cedar Rapids (IA) Gazette,* February 14, 1999, http://www.gazettconline.com (article no longer available).

2. "George Washington Carver," April 27, 2002, http://web.mit.edu/invent/iow/carver.html (accessed December 15, 2010).

3. "George Washington Carver," February 23, 2002, http://www.biography.com (article no longer available).

4. Merck, "Mectizan Program Removes Darkness from an Ancient Disease," *Corporate Philanthropy Report,* April 27, 2002, http://www.merck.com (no longer available).

5. Philippians 2:3–4 (New International Version).

Chapter 11. Rely on Bottom-Line Thinking

1. John A. Byrne, "Profiting from the Non-profits," *BusinessWeek,* March 26, 1990, 70.

2. Ibid., 72.

3. "Hesselbein Wins Presidential Medal of Freedom," December 19, 2001, http://www.drucker.org.

ABOUT THE AUTHOR

JOHN C. MAXWELL is an internationally recognized leadership expert, speaker, coach, and author who has sold over nineteen million books. Dr. Maxwell is the founder of EQUIP and the John Maxwell Company, organizations that have trained more than five million leaders worldwide. Every year he speaks to *Fortune* 500 companies, international government leaders, and organizations as diverse as the U.S. Military Academy at West Point, the National Football League, and the United Nations. A *New York Times*, *Wall Street Journal*, and *Business Week* bestselling author, Maxwell has written three books that have each sold more than one million copies: *The 21 Irrefutable Laws of Leadership*, *Developing the Leader Within You*, and *The 21 Indispensable Qualities of a Leader*. You can find him at JohnMaxwell.com and follow him at Twitter.com/ JohnCMaxwell.

PLEASE TURN THE PAGE FOR A PREVIEW OF

JOHN C. MAXWELL

THE

5

LEVELS

OF

LEADERSHIP

PROVEN STEPS TO MAXIMIZE YOUR POTENTIAL

THE 5 LEVELS OF LEADERSHIP IS THE TOPIC FORTUNE 100 COMPANIES ASK JOHN MAXWELL TO SPEAK ON MORE THAN ANY OTHER. NOW HE SHARES THE SECRETS OF EACH STAGE AND HOW YOU CAN GROW THROUGH EACH ONE TO REACH YOUR MAXIMUM POTENTIAL AND INFLUENCE.

Coming from Center Street
October 2011

CENTER
STREET

LEVEL 1 — POSITION

It's a Great Place to Visit, But You Wouldn't Want to Live There

Leadership traditionally begins with Position. Someone joins the army, and he or she becomes a recruit, working to earn the rank of private. A person gets a job, and along with it usually comes a title or job description: laborer, salesperson, waiter, clerk, accountant, manager. Position is the starting place for every level of leadership. It is the bottom floor and the foundation upon which leadership must be built. Real influence must be developed upon that foundation.

There was a time when people relied heavily on position to lead, which is no surprise when you consider that, at one time, hereditary leadership positions were handed down within families, from father to son (and sometimes daughter). Princes became kings and their decisions were law — for good or bad. In most industrialized nations, those days are gone. True, there are still nations with kings and queens, but even in most of those nations, such as England, monarchs rule with the permission of the people, and the real leaders are usually elected. Position gives you a chance, but it usually carries with it very little real power, except in systems where the penalties for not following are dire.

There's nothing wrong with having a *position* of leadership. When a person receives a leadership position, it's usually because someone in authority saw talent and potential in that person. And with that title and position come some rights and a degree of authority to lead others.

Position is a good starting place. And like every level of leadership, it has its upsides and downsides.

THE UPSIDE OF POSITION: YOU HAVE BEEN INVITED TO THE LEADERSHIP TABLE

Just as there are positive and negative aspects in every season of life, there are both positive and negative aspects to every level of leadership. If you are new to leadership and you receive a position, then there are things to celebrate. I'm going to tell you about four of them.

1. A Leadership Position Is Usually Given to People Because They Have Leadership Potential

Most of the time when people enter a leadership position, they do so because it was granted or they were appointed by some other person in authority. That probably seems obvious. But think about the implications: It usually means that the person in authority believes that the new leader has some degree of potential for leading. That's good news. So if you're new to leadership and you have been invited to lead something, then celebrate the fact that someone in authority believes in you.

If you have a new leadership position, then let me say welcome to the first step in your leadership journey. You have a seat at the table and have been invited to be part of the "leadership game." You will have opportunities to express your opinion and make decisions. Your initial goal should be to show your leader and your team that you deserve the position you have received.

2. A Leadership Position Means Authority Is Recognized

When an individual receives a position and title, some level of authority or power usually comes with them. Often in the beginning that power is very limited, but that's okay because most leaders need to prove themselves with little before being given much. As the *Infantryman's Journal* (1954) says, "No man is a leader until his appointment is ratified in the minds and the hearts of his men."

As a new leader, you must use wisely the authority you are given, to advance the team and help the people you lead. Do that, and your people will begin to give you even greater authority. When that happens, you gain leadership, not just a position.

3. A Leadership Position Is an Invitation to Grow as a Leader

There should always be a relationship between receiving a leadership position and fulfilling the requirements demanded by it. One of the main requirements is personal growth. I learned this early in my life from my father, who loved to quote, "To whoever much is given, much shall be required." He believed that each of us had received a lot in life, and we had a responsibility to learn and grow so that we could make the most of it.

The journey through the Five Levels of Leadership will only be successful if you dedicate yourself to continual development. If you believe that the position makes the leader, you will have a hard time becoming a good leader. You will be tempted to stop and "graze," meaning you'll stay where you are and enjoy the position's benefits, instead of striving to grow and become the best leader you can.

4. A Leadership Position Allows Potential Leaders to Shape and Define Their Leadership

The greatest potential upside for people invited to take a leadership position is that it affords them the opportunity to decide what kind of leader they want to be. The position they receive may be defined, but *they* are not.

When you first become a leader, your leadership page is blank and you get to fill it in any way you want! What kind of leader do you want to be? Don't just become reactive and develop a style by default. Really think about it. Do you want to be a tyrant or a team builder? Do you want to come down on people or lift them up? Do you want to give orders or ask questions? You can develop whatever style you want as long as it is consistent with who you are.

As you think about the way you will define your leadership, take into consideration what kinds of habits and systems you will consistently practice. What will you do to organize yourself? What will you do every day when you arrive at work? What spiritual practices will you maintain to keep yourself on track? How will you treat people? What will be your work ethic? What kind of example will you set? Everything is up for grabs. It's up to you to define it. And the earlier you are in your leadership journey, the greater the potential for gain if you start developing good habits now.

The bottom line is that an invitation to lead people is an invitation to make a difference. Good leadership changes individual lives. It forms teams. It builds organizations. It impacts communities. It has the potential to impact the world. But never forget that position is only the starting point.

THE DOWNSIDE OF POSITION:
TRUE LEADERSHIP ISN'T ABOUT POSITION

Like everything else in life, the Position level of leadership has negatives as well as positives. Each of the levels of leadership possesses downsides as well as upsides. You will find as you move up the levels that the upsides increase and the downsides decrease. Since Position is the lowest level of leadership, it has a great number of negatives. On Level 1, I see eight major downsides:

1. Having a Leadership Position Is Often Misleading

The easiest way to define leadership is by position. Once you have a position or title, people will identify you with it. However, positions and titles are very misleading. A position always promises more than it can deliver.

2. Leaders Who Rely on Position to Lead Often Devalue People

People who rely on position for their leadership almost always place a very high value on holding onto their position — often above everything else they do. Their position is more important to them than the work they do, the value they add to their subordinates, or their contribution to the organization. This kind of attitude does nothing to promote good relationships with people. In fact, positional leaders often see subordinates as an annoyance, as interchangeable cogs in the organizational machine, or even as troublesome obstacles to their goal of getting a promotion to their next position. As a result, departments, teams, or organizations that have positional leaders suffer terrible morale.

3. Positional Leaders Feed on Politics

When leaders value position over the ability to influence others, the environment of the organization usually becomes very political. There is a lot of maneuvering. Positional leaders focus on control instead of contribution. They work to gain titles. They do what they can to get the largest staff and the biggest budget they can — not for the sake of the organization's mission, but for the sake of expanding and defending their turf. And when a positional leader is able to do this, it often incites others to do the same because they worry that others' gains will be their loss. Not only does it create a vicious cycle of gamesmanship, posturing, and maneuvering, but it also creates departmental rivalries and silos.

4. Positional Leaders Place Rights Over Responsibilities

Poet T.S. Eliot asserted, "Half of the harm that is done in this world is due to people who want to feel important...they do not mean to do harm...they are absorbed in the endless struggle to think well of themselves." That's what positional leaders do: they do things to make themselves look and feel important.

Inevitably, positional leaders who rely on their rights develop a sense of entitlement. They expect their people to serve them, rather than looking for ways to serve their people. Their job description is more important to them than job development. They value territory over teamwork. As a result, they usually emphasize rules and regulations that are to their advantage and they ignore relationships. This does nothing to promote teamwork and create a positive working environment.

Just because you have the right to do something as a leader doesn't mean that it is the right thing to do. Changing your focus from rights to responsibilities is often a sign of maturity in a leader.

5. Positional Leadership Is Often Lonely

Positional leaders can become lonely if they misunderstand the functions and purpose of leadership. Being a good leader doesn't mean trying to be king of the hill and standing above (and set apart) from others. Good leadership is about walking beside people and helping them to climb up the hill with you. If you're atop the hill alone, you may get lonely. If you have others alongside you, it's hard to be that way.

6. Leaders Who Remain Positional Get Branded and Stranded

Whenever people use their position to lead others for an extended period of time and fail to develop genuine influence, they become branded as positional leaders, and they rarely get further opportunities for advancement in that organization. They may move laterally, but they rarely move up.

If you have been a positional leader, you can change, and this book will help you. However, you need to recognize that the longer you have relied on your position, the more difficult it will be for you to change others' perception about your leadership style. You may even need to change positions in order to restart the process of developing influence with others.

7. Turnover Is High for Positional Leaders

When people rely on their positions for leadership, the result is almost always high turnover. In my book *Leadership Gold*, one of the chapters is titled "People Quit People, Not Companies." In it I explain how people often take a job because they want to be part of a particular company, but when they quit it's almost always because they want to get away from particular people.

Every company has turnover. It is inevitable. The question every leader must ask is, "Who is leaving?" Organizations with Level 1 leadership tend to lose their best people and attract average or below-average people. The more Level 1 leaders an organization has, the more the door swings out with high-level people and in with low-level ones.

8. Positional Leaders Receive People's Least, Not Their Best

People who rely on their positions and titles are the weakest of all leaders. They give their least. They expect their position to do the hard work for them in leadership. As a result, their people also give their least. Some people who work for a positional leader may start out strong, ambitious, innovative, and motivated, but they rarely stay that way.

The greatest downside to Level 1 leadership is that it is neither creative nor innovative. It's leadership that just gets by. And if a leader stays on the *downside* of Level 1 long enough, he may find himself on the *outside*. If a leader fails on Level 1, there's nowhere to go but U-Haul territory. He'll be moving out and looking for another job.